130

BIBLICAL DEVOTIONS

C. Keith Mee

CROSSBOOKS
PUBLISHING

CrossBooks™
A Division of LifeWay
1663 Liberty Drive
Bloomington, IN 47403
www.crossbooks.com
Phone: 1-866-879-0502

*Unless otherwise indicated, Scripture passages are taken from the New American Standard
Bible, copyright 1960, 1962, 1963, 1968, 1971, 1972, 1973, and 1975 by the Lockman
Foundation or from the Holman Christian Standard Bible, copyright 2010 by Holman
Bible Publishers as indicated by "HCSB" after each reference. Both used by permission.*

First published by CrossBooks 05/22/2012

ISBN: 978-1-4627-1683-8 (sc)
ISBN: 978-1-4627-1685-2 (hc)
ISBN: 978-1-4627-1684-5 (e)

Library of Congress Control Number: 2012906876

Printed in the United States of America

This book is printed on acid-free paper.

*Any people depicted in stock imagery provided by Thinkstock are models,
and such images are being used for illustrative purposes only.*

Certain stock imagery © Thinkstock.

Contents

INTRODUCTION

These 130 biblical devotionals were first presented to a senior adult department at Central Baptist Church Bearden, in Knoxville, Tennessee. My wife, Jean, and I are codirectors of the department. I have tried to make the devotionals Bible centered.

We have included the following areas: beliefs, the Ten Commandments, the Beatitudes, the fruit of the Spirit, holidays, God and Jesus, things seen through God's eyes, the little word *if,* prophecies, Psalm 23, faith and love, and a miscellaneous section labeled others.

At the end of each devotional, I have included a place for notes. My hope is that the book might be used for Bible study and that the reader will add ideas, questions, and comments.

Also, I hope the book might be used for devotionals in some other settings. I think pastors might find the devotionals helpful as sermon ideas or starters.

I have included illustrations from my own life with the hope that family and friends might find these helpful. I have tried to give credit for quotes and wording. My apologies if I have overlooked anyone. The background of information and understanding comes from sixty-five years of Bible study, teaching, listening to thousands of sermons, and reading hundreds of books.

My sons David and Bobby were especially helpful in showing me how to use Word on the computer.

I am grateful for all the patient help given me by the people at CrossBooks Publishing.

Keith Mee, Knoxville, Tennessee

IT?

IT IS FINISHED!

What did Jesus mean in John 19:30 (HCSB) when He said, "It is finished"? Jesus obviously did not mean "I am finished." Other translations word the phrase as *all is finished, the task is done.* The *it* could mean a lot of things, such as "everything is now completed," "all is done," or "My mission is over." So what, then, does the statement mean?

The Broadman Bible Commentary[1] explains *it* this way: "The exclamation may have been heard by the bystanders as a sigh of resignation, an acknowledgement that His cause was finished. The believing reader, however, cannot help but hear an exclamation that the epoch of redemption had reached its climax, that Jesus, 'Having loved His own who were in the world, He loved them to the end' (John 13:1b HCSB). Now every man can take hope not on the basis of his frustrated sense of incompleteness but on the basis of the finished work of Christ."

The first clue to God's plan is found in Genesis, where, after Adam and Eve had sinned, God said to Satan, "I will put hostility between you and the woman, and between your seed and her seed. He will strike your head, and you will strike His heel" (Genesis 3:15 HCSB). Jesus fulfilled this prophecy on the cross when He rescued us from Satan's power.

Much of the rest of the Bible explains or pictures in many ways how God would provide for our salvation. "For the life of a creature is in the blood, and I have appointed it to you to make atonement on the altar for your lives, since it is the life*blood* that makes atonement" (Leviticus 17:11 HCSB, emphasis mine). The New Testament says, "According to the law almost everything is purified with blood, and without the shedding of blood there is no forgiveness" (Hebrews 9:22 HCSB).

Much of Scripture's attempt to portray what was required for sin to be forgiven was the animal sacrifices that were done in the tabernacle and later in the temple. These pictured what one day Christ would do on the cross to make our salvation possible: "But he was pierced because of our transgressions, crushed because of our iniquities; punishment for our peace was on Him, and we are healed by His wounds" (Isaiah 53:5 HCSB).

"He made the One who did not know sin to be sin for us so that we might become the righteousness of God in Him" (2 Corinthians 5:21 HCSB).

Without the shedding of blood, there would be no way our sin could be forgiven. Perhaps this is God's way of impressing on man the seriousness of sin. The shedding of Jesus' innocent blood, to make possible the forgiveness of sin, is *God's great gift* to mankind: "For the wages of sin is death, but the gift of God is eternal life in Christ Jesus our Lord" (Romans 6:23 HCSB).

The story of redemption that the Bible explains, pictures, prophesies, and dramatizes from Genesis to Revelation, the message of salvation for all who believe, is the *it!*

Notes

Beliefs Matter

Beliefs

In his book *The Divine Conspiracy*[2] Dallas Willard makes a statement about beliefs: "We often speak of people not living up to their faith. But the cases in which we say this are not really cases of people behaving other than they believe. They are cases in which genuine beliefs are made obvious by what people do. We always live up to our beliefs or down to them, as the case may be. Nothing else is possible. It is the nature of beliefs."

What Willard says is at least one of the reasons why we have so many church members absent from worship services and Bible study. It explains why thousands give little or nothing in support of their churches. It explains why it is difficult to get workers for vacation Bible school and other church ministries. Beliefs matter! If a person really believes that the church is the body of Christ and that loyalty and service to the church is the way he or she is loyal to Christ, then he or she will support the church in every possible way.

Jesus said, "You will know them by their fruits. Grapes are not gathered from thorn bushes, nor figs from thistles, are they? So then, you will know them by their fruits" (Matthew 7:16, 20). John reminds us, "If you love Me, you will keep my commandments" (John 14:15). Jesus said, "I will build My church" (Matthew 16:18). As Christians, we get our beliefs from the Bible. Of course, belief determines how seriously we take the Bible. Our beliefs depend on how well we know and believe the Bible.

Once, I was invited to speak to a group of students at the University of Kentucky. They were having a series of lectures on what different denominations believe. My assignment was to tell them what Baptists believe. This was difficult, because there are about fifty different Baptist denominations. I did my best to tell them what Southern Baptists believe. Then I let them ask questions. After several questions, the student leader said, "What you have said is all well and good, but you have based everything on the Bible, and everyone knows that the Bible is a dead book."

For many people, the Bible may not be a dead book, but it is an ignored book. Some of us pick and choose which parts to believe. Still others know what it means but excuse themselves from the actions and attitudes it prescribes. Beliefs matter because they control our lives. "One man regards one day above another, another regards every day alike. Let each man be fully convinced in his own mind" (Romans 14:5). To be convinced in our own mind, about any matter, is what we really believe about that matter, and what we really believe about that matter controls what we do about it, whether it be church attendance, service opportunities, stewardship, prayer, Bible study, faithfulness to our spouse, honesty, or gossip.

When we are saved, everything we think we know about what is wrong is not corrected immediately. We spend the rest of our lives learning what is wrong and what God's will is about things. It is called sanctification or Christian growth. "So then, my beloved, just as you have always obeyed, not as in my presence only, but now much more in my absence, work out your own salvation with fear and trembling; for it is God who is at work in you, both to will and to work for His good pleasure" (Philippians 2:12–13). Romans adds, "And do not be conformed to this world, but be transformed by the renewing of your mind, that you may prove what the will of God is, that which is good and acceptable and perfect" (Romans 12:2).

Scripture tells us to be of one mind. The apostle Paul gives this advice: "Now the God who gives perseverance and encouragement grant you to be of the same mind with one another according to Christ Jesus; That with one accord you may with one voice glorify the God and Father of our Lord Jesus Christ" (Romans 15:5).

Notes

BELIEFS MATTER NO. 2

I have a book titled *Belief Matters,*[3] by Pete Briscoe. He is the son of well-known authors Stuart and Jill Briscoe. I have been trying to figure out the difference between the title to my series, *Beliefs Matter,* and the title of his book *Belief Matters.* The words of both titles are true, of course, but it seems to me that specific beliefs are what really matter rather than belief in general. Briscoe explains why belief is important. He writes, "Belief matters. It is quite impossible to overemphasize that fact. Belief determines our perceptions of reality. Belief shapes every thought, decision, and action. Belief defines the limits of what is possible. Belief emerges from the soul—from that inner core of our being that defines who we are and what we do."

Belief is defined as "to accept as true or real." Beliefs are specific convictions, doctrines, or assumptions that determine our actions and decisions. The radical Muslim believes that if he martyrs himself, killing those who aren't Muslims, he'll go to heaven and be given virgins.

Read *Foxe's Book of Martyrs* about how people were burned at the stake because they refused to renounce their faith in Christ alone for salvation rather than depending on the Catholic Church.

Scripture tells us very specifically of some critical beliefs. For example, "For God so loved the world, that He gave His only begotten Son, that whoever believes in Him should not perish, but have eternal life" (John 3:16). We can accept that this is true mentally but do nothing that a genuine belief would require. For us to have confidence that our belief is real there would need to be some evidence that a change had taken place in our life.

Jesus tells Martha, "I am the resurrection and the life; He who believes in me shall live even if he dies, and everyone who lives and believes in Me shall never die" (John 11:25–26). If this verse is to mean anything to the believer, the person would have to have knowledge of other Scripture. Bible study is absolutely necessary if the Christian is to appreciate what Jesus meant by never dying.

"If you confess with your mouth Jesus as Lord, and believe in your heart that God raised Him from the dead, you shall be saved; for with the heart man believes, resulting in righteousness, and with the mouth he confesses, resulting in salvation" (Romans 10:9–10).

Jesus said, "He who has my commandments and keeps them, he it is who loves me; and he who loves Me shall be loved by My Father, and

I will love him, and will disclose myself to him" (John 14:21). Having Jesus' commandments implies spending time in Bible study and prayer to determine just what it is Jesus expects of us. Having beliefs and keeping them are two different things. James cautioned, "Therefore, to one who knows the right thing to do, and does not do it, to him it is sin" (James 4:17). Spending time with other believers, in Bible study and prayer, will help us make the decisions to do the right thing. We need the encouragement and example of other believers to help us do that.

The opposite of belief and trust is doubt or skepticism. Living with doubt is hard. A person has to be wondering if all is well. He may feel free from the restraints that belief in God would impose, but he doesn't have the joy and peace of mind that comes from forgiveness of sin and the confidence that when he dies, he'll be safe in the arms of Jesus Christ.

Notes

LOVE

"You shall love the Lord God with all your heart, and with all your soul, and with your entire mind. This is the great and foremost commandment. And the second is like it; you shall love your neighbor as yourself" (Matthew 22:37–39). Agape love means that we are to do that which is in the best interest of our neighbor and of the Lord. When Jesus was asked, "Who is my neighbor?" He told the story of the Good Samaritan. I take this to mean that our neighbor is anyone in need of help.

The word *Lord* occurs in the Bible 7,900 times. *Love* occurs 358 times, *yourself* 587 times, and *neighbor* 148 times. Who then are we to love? In Romans 12:20 we are told to do well, even to our enemy. With that extreme in mind, we should love everyone, even those who do us dirt, and especially everyone in the body of Christ, the church.

How do we love? "Blessed be the God and Father of our Lord Jesus Christ, the Father of mercies and God of all comfort; who comforts us in all of our afflictions so that we may be able to comfort those who are in any affliction with the comfort with which we ourselves are comforted by God" (2 Corinthians 1:3–4). The word *comfort* can mean "to encourage." The more we have experienced God's help ourselves, the better able we are to help others. Our prayer life and our Bible study make us more aware of God's involvement in our life, and this in turn equips us to encourage others.

Here are some of the reasons why people need encouragement: ruptured relationships, job difficulties, health problems, money, loneliness, feeling inferior, family conflicts, and loss of a loved one or a friend. The more we know about people, the more we are able to know how to encourage them. Some of us are bashful and not too adept at taking the initiative. This can be changed if we push ourselves a little and get some practice.

When we meet people, there is a good chance that most of them can use a little dose of encouragement: a smile, a pat on the back, a listening ear, a compliment. We may not be aware of it, but even pastors, teachers, and other leaders need encouragement rather than criticism. After I was saved, I started complimenting my pastor regularly. Many pastors get more criticism than they do compliments. We can love by encouraging each other: "And be kind to one another, tender-hearted, forgiving each other, just as God in Christ also has forgiven you" (Ephesians 4:32).

My first wife, Carol, was a caring person. At a fellowship she would go to people she saw standing alone and talk to them. Too many of us get with our friends and don't even notice the stranger or the "wallflower." It seemed that women who were not in the "popular" crowd would gravitate toward Carol. Her nature reminds me of a verse of Scripture: "Be of the same mind toward one another; do not be haughty in mind, but associate with the lowly. Do not be wise in your own estimation" (Romans 12:16).

Part of our responsibility is being alert to the needs of others. There are many people who were once active in church but now are missing. It is the responsibility of every active Christian to be aware of those who are missing and take steps to find out why. Organization is good and necessary, but everyone should feel the need to help.

There is a song titled "Love Is the Theme." The chorus includes the phrase "love is supreme." In the Christian community there is nothing more important than *love* in action.

Notes

Salvation No. 1

Hebrews 2:3 asks, "How shall we escape if we neglect such a great salvation?" There is no escaping an eternity in hell for those who turn down God's gift of salvation through Jesus Christ.

There are other consequences of neglect. Good news ceases to be good news for people who treat lightly the best news that ever came out of heaven. Neglect can take many forms. Some may think their public profession of faith was all that was involved. Others may think of salvation simply as a way of escaping hell and gaining heaven and nothing more.

For salvation to be what God intended requires us to study His word and respond positively to its demands. A verse that many of us learned in Training Union is "Be diligent to present yourself approved to God as a workman who does not need to be ashamed, handling accurately the word of truth" (2 Timothy 2:15). The King James Bible tells us to *study*. Whichever we choose, to be diligent or to study, we are admonished to be acquainted with biblical expectations and respond positively to their requirements.

A way of mishandling the Bible is to accept what we like and ignore its demands. One such verse is in Ephesians: "For by grace you have been saved through faith; and that not of yourselves, it is the gift of God; not as a result of works that no one should boast. For we are His workmanship, created in Christ Jesus for good works, which God prepared beforehand, that we should walk in them" (Ephesians 2:8–10). Some people ignore God's expectation that we would *walk in good works*.

The good works of verse 10 are what give evidence that we have really been saved. Without the good works of verse 10, there will be no growth as a Christian. The good works of verse 10 help us to appreciate many of God's promises. Some Christians start off strong but the cares of the world or the attraction of material things dampens their zeal for service and stewardship. Such would be neglect of their salvation.

Salvation should result in the fruit of the Spirit, which are love, joy, peace, patience, kindness, goodness, and faithfulness. Neglect of salvation results in just the opposite, such as selfishness, jealousy, critical spirit, pride, and impatience.

The greatness of salvation should become more real for us as we realize the significance of Christ's sacrifice and as we learn what God has in store for His adopted children. Now He sees us as though we have never sinned, because He has replaced our sin with the righteousness of Christ.

We grow as we come to appreciate the church and our fellowship with fellow believers. We grow as we experience God's answers to prayer and His protection. More and more we learn what it means to be adopted into God's family and to have the privilege of addressing the Creator of the universe as Daddy, brother, and friend.

As we serve out our salvation instead of neglecting it, we experience the joy of our salvation more and more. As we experience the joy of our salvation, it gives our witness a glow that enables us to be more effective in winning others to Christ.

Salvation is so much more than a ticket to heaven. We'll never discover that "so much more" unless we are faithful in Bible study, prayer, and church attendance.

Notes

SALVATION NO. 2

There is probably no more important word in our language than *salvation*. No other word is more abused, misunderstood, debated, preached, and taught. No other word is the key, the means, the way, and the hope for an eternity in heaven. The very word implies that we need to be saved. It suggests that our future is in jeopardy and that danger lies ahead. It also suggests that someone or something has the means or ability to save us. If we were told that we were lost, without any way of being found, life would be bleak indeed.

"Blessed be the Lord God of Israel, for He has visited us and accomplished redemption for His people, and has raised up a horn of salvation for us in the house of David His servant" (Luke 1:68–69). Only a sick person needs a doctor. Only a lost person needs to be found. To be spiritually lost is to be separated from God our Creator. Everyone has sinned, and sin, unless removed, comes between us and our Creator.

There are many false means of salvation—false because they don't take away our sin. Some of these are church membership, good works, keeping the law, and living by the Golden Rule. God says in His word, "Without the shedding of blood there is no forgiveness" (Hebrews 9:22b). God has provided the way to remove the sin and thus to make a way for man to have fellowship with Him. The shed blood that is required for the forgiveness of sin is the innocent, sinless blood of Christ: "For this is my blood of the covenant, which is to be shed on behalf of many for forgiveness of sins" (Matthew 26:28).

"...knowing that you were not redeemed with perishable things like silver and gold from your futile way of life inherited from your forefathers, but with the precious blood, of a lamb unblemished and spotless, the blood of Christ" (1 Peter 1:18–19). How do we acquire the benefit of Christ's shed blood? There are many words related to salvation. Some of them are *conversion, reconciliation, propitiation, remission, redemption, regeneration, adoption, justification, sanctification,* and *glorification*. These pretty well cover all facets of salvation.

The initial and most crucial is the first, *conversion,* which involves repentance and faith. Jesus said, "Unless you are converted and become as little children, you shall not enter the kingdom of heaven" (Matthew 8:3). Repentance is a sincere turning from sin. The crucial sin is the rejection of Christ, not believing who He said He is. "He who believes in Him is not judged; he who does not believe has been judged already, because he has not believed in the name of the only begotten Son of God" (John 3:18). This requires faith. "So then faith comes by hearing, and hearing by the word of Christ" (Romans 10:17). Realization that I am a lost sinner is caused by the work of the Holy Spirit. "And He, when He comes, will convict the world concerning sin, and righteousness, and judgment; concerning sin, because they do not believe in Me" (John 16:8–9).

Now we come to the best-known verse in the Bible: "For God so loved the world that He gave His only begotten Son, that whoever believes in Him should not perish, but have eternal life" (John 3:16). Justification is the beginning of salvation. Sanctification or Christian life is next, and glorification is the climax as we join Christ and our loved ones in heaven.

Recently, at our church, we were treated to a beautiful rendition of "Amazing Grace." The soloist said, "This song has been sung in every language on earth." How wonderful that is, if it is true, but many still have not heard it, and many who have heard it have not responded. We must remain at the task of witnessing to the lost in this world.

Jesus Paid It All[4]
Jesus paid it all, all to Him I owe,
Sin had left a crimson stain
He washed it white as snow.

Notes

GRACE-FAITH-WORKS

My source for thoughts on this subject is *Baptist Distinctives*[5] by W. R. White. There is a lot of misunderstanding or difference of opinion about these three words. Is salvation all of faith based on grace? Or is it all of works or a combination of faith and works? Here is a key Bible verse that contains all three words: "For by grace you have been saved through faith; and that not of yourselves, it is the gift of God; not as a result of works, that no one should boast. For we are His workmanship, created in Christ Jesus for good works, which God prepared beforehand that we should walk in them" (Ephesians 2:8–10).

White says, "Salvation by grace is the only possible salvation for depraved man. At his best he falls short of the glory of God. All admit that there must be some extension of mercy. It would be impossible for man to know when he had the proper proportion of grace and works if salvation depended on a combination of works and grace. Someone will say 'Just do your best and depend on God's mercy for the rest'. But no one does his best every minute for any considerable period of time.

Besides, we are so human that when we do some very godly "deed, subtle forces of selfishness and carnality may greatly influence our motives without our being conscious of it. In the very nature of the case, salvation has to be all of works or all of grace." "But if it is by grace, it is no longer on the basis of works, otherwise grace is no longer grace (Romans 11:6)."

This reminds me of a statement made many years ago at a Baptist Student Union convention in Lexington, Kentucky. The speaker, Andy Blane, said, "We never do any good deed for a totally unselfish motive. We either do it to avoid feeling guilty or after we have done it we feel proud of ourselves."

It is important to know without any doubt that we are depending on God's grace and not on anything we have done or are doing for our salvation.

Salvation is, according to the Bible, a gift—you don't work for a gift. "For the wages of sin is death, but the free gift of God is eternal life in Christ Jesus our Lord" (Romans 6:23). Works are the result of salvation and not the means of salvation. White[6] says, "Due to the weakness of human nature the Lord has provided certain disciplines. Those who disobey are chastised but not disowned or cast out of the redeemed family. Those who are faithful are rewarded." "Watch yourselves that you might not lose what we have accomplished, but that you may receive a full reward" (2 John 8). Also there is this verse: "My son, do not regard lightly the discipline of the Lord" (Hebrews 12: 5). We must be careful not to let pride, logic or any other influence cause us to depend on anything other than God's grace and our faith to save us and keep us.

Some may take Jesus' statement in Matthew 25:31–46 to mean that the good work of visiting the sick and feeding the poor is what saves us and failing to do so is what condemns us. To give this meaning to the passage would contradict many other passages of Scripture. Feeding the poor and visiting the sick is good work, but we are not saved by our good works. For me the only possible meaning is that when we are saved, we do these good works. Failure to do them can be evidence that we are really not saved.

Notes

MAN

"And God created man in His own image, in the image of God He created him; male and female He created them" (Genesis 1:27). We are the result of divine creativity, not the result of mindless matter. No amount of matter, mixed by forces of nature over any amount of time, can produce patterns, let alone life. The second law of thermodynamics says that the mixing of matter homogenizes that matter. The mixing of matter does not produce patterns.

Living matter, even in its simplest forms, is a very complex pattern. In the Psalms 139:14, David says: "I will give thanks to Thee, for I am fearfully and wonderfully made." In a book[7] by that name the author, Dr. Paul Brand, tells us: "if our DNA were extracted and compacted together, it would occupy a space the size of an ice cube. If that DNA were stretched out end to end, it would reach to the sun and back 400 times." How could anything be more amazing than that? Our bodies are truly complex.

Our blood constitutes about thirty pounds or nearly one fifth of our weight. The heart is six inches in length and four inches in diameter. It beats 2½ billion times in seventy years. All the blood in our body passes through the heart once every three minutes. Every day our heart beats equal in work to lifting a one-ton weight 122 feet. The Bible says, "The life of all flesh is in the blood" (Leviticus 17:14b).

God made us body, soul, and spirit. Some theologians equate soul and spirit. In a few places in the Bible, the two are used interchangeably. Lower animals have soul and body but not spirit. In any case He made people in His image. The crucial part of us is our brain, which stores knowledge, thinks creatively, and makes decisions. Adam and Eve made a bad decision and disobeyed God. Thus sin entered the world, separated man from God, and was passed through Adam to all men.

God made us for Himself. He desires our love and devotion. For that to be meaningful it had to be freely given. For that to occur, God gave us free will. God also gave us responsibility. He said, "Be fruitful and multiply, and fill the earth, and subdue it; and rule over the fish of the sea and the birds of the sky, and over every living thing that moves on the earth" (Genesis 1:28).

Adam and Eve's sin severed the relationship they had with God. Throughout the Old Testament and into the New, God worked to make a way for men to come back to Him. He formed a nation of people to be the way through which this help would come. In spite of all the work God did to prepare them for what He would do, when that plan came into fruition, most of those people didn't recognize Him. "He came to His own, and those who were His own did not receive Him. But as many as received Him, to them He gave the right to become children of God, even to those who believe in His name" (John 1:11–12). His plan reached its climax with Jesus' death and resurrection.

Jesus set about building His church. He called Saul, who became Paul. Among His last words were "Go therefore and make disciples of all the nations" (Matthew 28:19). After Jesus ascended into heaven, the Holy Spirit was given to His followers and churches began to be formed. That is where we are today, working and waiting for His return and a whole new world.

We are engaged in God's plan for the world. We are personally accountable for doing our part as God leads. "The fear of the Lord is the beginning of wisdom; a good understanding has all those who do His commandments; His praise endures forever" (Psalm 111:10).

Notes

Soul Competency

"Look to the rock from which you are hewn" (Isaiah 51:1b). This is a call to focus our hearts and minds on the basic principles that characterize our faith. Obviously there are certain beliefs that make us Baptists. The most basic of these beliefs, according to E. Y. Mullins, in *The Baptist Faith and Message,* is the competency of the soul in religion. The following several paragraphs are adapted from *The Baptist Faith and Message:*[8]

The competency of the soul in religion means competency under God, not self-sufficiency. God created people in His own image. He endowed us with understanding and the privilege of choice. This is called free will. People are not puppets. God does not force us against our will. We are free to choose but we are responsible for our choices.

Soul competency excludes human interference in our religious life such as rule by bishops, religious proxy (no one can act in our behalf) and governmental authority in religion. Religion is a personal matter between the soul and God. Mullins lists an expansion of this soul competency. God is sovereign, everyone has equal and direct access to God, we have equal privileges in the church, to be responsible we must be free, a free church in a free state, and we are to love our neighbors as ourselves.

Although we believe in soul competency, Baptists insist on some specific beliefs such as the Lordship of Jesus Christ and the authority of the Scriptures. We also believe that everyone is free to decide for himself whether to be a Baptist, a Methodist, a Jew, an atheist, or nothing. God doesn't coerce us, and we don't have the right to coerce others in matters of religion.

We are a priesthood of believers. "You are a chosen race, a Royal Priesthood, a Holy Nation, a people for God's own possession, that you may proclaim the excellences of Him who has called you out of darkness into His marvelous light" (1 Peter 2:9). Everyone has a right to his own opinion that is probably why there are some fifty different Baptist denominations.

Scripture requires us to work out our differences to preserve the unity within the body. In Ephesians Paul writes: "I, therefore, the prisoner of the Lord, entreat you to walk in a manner worthy of the calling with which you have been called, with all humility and gentleness, with patience, showing forbearance to one another in love, being diligent to preserve the unity of the Spirit in the bond of peace" (Ephesians 4:1–3). People get along just so long as they submit to the Lordship of Christ and the authority of the Scriptures.

We are free to love God and trust Him to provide for us now and for the future. God could have made us like puppets or like the animals of the field that function by instinct, but our love of Him would have been meaningless. Love has meaning only when it is freely given. It cannot be demanded or coerced. If we had been made like the animals of the field, there would have been no creativity, no one to appreciate the beauty of creation or to care for it, and no utilization of the treasures of the earth. Life is truly meaningful only to the extent that we live and work in partnership with our Creator.

Notes

Justification, Sanctification, Glorification

C. B. Hogue, in his book, *The Doctrine of Salvation,*[9] says, "The changes produced by salvation are so numerous, so radical, and so far-reaching that no single word or phrase can describe them all fully." We are looking briefly at three key words involved in salvation. The first of these is *justification.* This is the "judicial act of God by which He declares the sinner to be free from condemnation and restores him to divine favor."[10] To be justified is for God to look upon those who are saved as though they had never sinned.

"For if by the transgression of the one the many died, much more did the grace of God and the gift by the grace of the one Man, Jesus Christ, abound to the many" (Romans 5:15). The gift of righteousness is the key. "He made Him who knew no sin to be sin on our behalf that we might become the righteousness of God in Him" (2 Corinthians 5–21). God sees the saved through the sinless life of our Lord Jesus.

After we have been justified, *sanctification* begins. We are set apart for God's service. We refer to it as Christian growth. Paul describes what takes place in the life of the saved: "I urge you therefore, brethren, by the mercies of God, to present your bodies a living and holy sacrifice, acceptable to God, which is your spiritual service of worship. And do not be conformed to this world, but be transformed by the renewing of your mind, that you may prove what the will of God is, that which is good and acceptable and perfect" (Romans 12:1–2).

When we are saved, we are spiritual babies. We have much to learn. The wrong notions and prejudices we have accumulated throughout life have to be discarded or changed as we study God's word and learn what His will is for our life. *Glorification* is one of the blessings awaiting the believer in the afterlife. "After you have suffered for a little while, the God of all grace, who called you to His eternal glory in Christ, will Himself perfect, confirm, strengthen and establish you" (1 Peter 5:10). Hogue says,[11] "Glorification means that the believer will be with Christ and will be like Him. The believer will participate in the final triumph and will be part of the endless ages."

"When Christ, who is our life, is revealed, then you also will be revealed with him in glory" (Colossians 3:4). Hogue continues: "Glorified believers will live in new and glorified bodies. They will be perfect in character and nature, freed at last from the weakness of the flesh." "Who (Jesus) will transform the body of our humble estate into conformity with the body of His glory, by the exertion of the power that He has even to subject all things to Himself" (Philippians 3:21).

Our job, as believers, is to grow in the faith and witness to the lost. As we grow in Bible knowledge and understanding, our witness should become more effective. God gives us at least one spiritual gift. We are responsible for discovering what it is and putting it to work helping to build up the body of Christ, the church. I recommend for study *19 Gifts of the Spirit*[12] by Leslie Flynn. This book can help you discover your spiritual gifts.

Notes

Jesus' Second Coming

I read an article recently that gave the reasons why the second coming of Jesus is eminent. It listed all of the events mentioned in Scripture that need to occur before Jesus' return. The article didn't set a date but simply claimed that most of what is supposed to happen before His return has happened.

The Baptist Faith and Message[13] makes this statement: "God in His own time and in His own way will bring the world to its appropriate end. According to His promise, Jesus will return personally and visibly in glory to the earth; the dead will be raised and Christ will judge all men in righteousness. The unrighteous will be consigned to Hell, the place of everlasting punishment. The righteous in their resurrected bodies will receive their reward and will dwell forever in Heaven with the Lord."

The apostle John records one of the most meaningful promises Jesus made: "Let not your heart be troubled; believe in God, believe also in Me. In my Father's house are many dwelling places; if it were not so, I would have told you; for I go to prepare a place for you. And if I go and prepare a place for you, I will come again, and receive you to Myself; that where I am, there you may be also" (John 14:1–3). When Carol, my first wife, died, this was the Scripture that meant the most to me. When she would be with Jesus was not a concern. In Jesus' own time, she would be with Him.

Whether Jesus comes immediately for the deceased person or at the end of time, I don't think the deceased person will be conscious of the passing of time. Matthew 24 gives us the most detail on things leading up to the end of time. When He says, "All the tribes of earth will see Him coming on clouds of the sky" (Matthew 24:30),it casts some doubt on His coming for each of us at the moment of our death. He has already come to each of us at the moment of our conversion where we have died to the old life and risen to a new life in Christ.

One verse that indicates we will be with Jesus at the moment of our death is Jesus' statement to the thief on the cross. Jesus said, "Truly I say to you, *today* you shall be with Me in Paradise" (Luke 23:43).

Jesus gives us the most specific condition that tells us when the second coming will occur: "And this gospel of the kingdom shall be preached in the whole world for a witness to all the nations, and then the end shall come" (Matthew 24:14). The most important consideration

---

concerning Jesus' second coming is that He *is* coming again. The only thing Christians can do to hasten that day is to share the gospel with all the nations.

We have been warned to be ready, because it will be sudden and without warning. There will be no time for lost people to be converted. The parable of the five foolish virgins tells us this. They went to get oil for their lamps but came back saying, "Lord, lord, open up for us. But He answered and said, 'Truly I say to you, I do not know you.' Be on the alert then, for you do not know the day nor the hour" (Matthew 25:11–13).

"Now may the God of peace Himself sanctify you entirely; and may your spirit and soul and body be preserved complete, without blame at the coming of our Lord Jesus Christ" (1 Thessalonians 5:23).

Our responsibility is to share the gospel with the lost. We can contribute to missions through our churches. We can pray for the missionaries. We are part of Jesus' team to help share the gospel with all the nations, beginning in our own communities.

"What a day that will be when our Jesus we shall see!"

Notes

Jesus' Fulfillment of Prophecy

We can't know the future except as God, through the prophets, has given us a glimpse of what is to come. Centuries ago He told the people of Israel what to expect. In spite of the miracles that God had done on their behalf, they disobeyed Him and continually complained about their situation. They were surrounded by enemies who finally took them captive.

Prophets, led by God, gave them hope for the future. These prophets spoke frequently about a coming redeemer. Much of the story from Genesis to Malachi alludes to His coming. The first was in Genesis where God said to the serpent, "And I will put enmity between you and the woman, and between your seed and her seed; He shall bruise you on the head, and you shall bruise him on the heel" (Genesis 3:15).

"Nearly all of the more than 300 prophesies have come true with only a few remaining for our future. One mathematician determined that the odds for one person's fulfilling even sixty specific prophesies are 1 in 1 plus 157 zeroes." (See 300 prophecies and 157 trillion on the internet) A thousand trillions has only fifteen zeroes. One in a number with 157 zeroes is synonymous with *impossible*.

Jesus' fulfillment of prophecy should convince any thinking person of His reality. Here are a few of the more well-known prophecies that He fulfilled.

"Therefore the Lord Himself will give you a sign: Behold, a virgin will be with child and bear a son, and she will call His name Immanuel" (Isaiah 7:14). Jesus was born of a virgin in Bethlehem just as was prophesied.

How could anyone read Isaiah 53 and not believe? "He was despised and rejected of men, a man of sorrows and acquainted with grief; He was pierced through for our transgressions, He was oppressed and He was afflicted, yet He opened not His mouth" (Isaiah 53:3, 5, 7). In this one chapter the pronouns *He, Him,* and *Himself* appear forty-six times. How could anyone read this without wondering who these words refer to?

Then there is Psalm 22: "My God, my God why hast thou forsaken me? They pierced my hands and my feet I can count all my bones. They look, they stare at me, they divide my garments among them, and for my clothing they cast lots" (Psalm 22:1, 16–18).

How about the specificity of prophecy in Micah: "But as for you, Bethlehem Ephrathah, too little to be among the clans of Judah, from you One will go forth for Me to be ruler of Israel. His goings forth are from long ago, from the days of eternity" (Micah 5:2).

Most important for us is the Messiah's mission as stated in Isaiah: "I will make you a light of the nation's so that my salvation may reach to the ends of the earth" (Isaiah 49:6b).

We are the most blessed of all people. God has seen fit to equip us with many translations of the Scriptures. There are thousands of churches and billions of believers. We are part of a massive spiritual army. Pray that in our generation we will complete the job of evangelizing the whole earth.

Notes

Jesus' Incarnation

Beliefs matter! They determine our attitudes and actions. If more evidence is needed, think of the five Americans who went to Pakistan, in 2009, planning to become martyrs. It matters about how strongly a person believes that Jesus is God become a man. As hard as it is to understand, it is true and must be accepted by faith.

God created the heavens and the Earth. God's creation is immense and beautiful. It consists of billions of galaxies. It is not only immense, but complex and beautiful. On the edge of this immense universe God created a really special place called Earth.

God wanted more than planets and stars, so He created life. God wanted more than life; He wanted a life form that could relate to Him in an intimate way. To accomplish this He created man. We are the beneficiaries of God's desire for companionship. How could a perfect, infinitely powerful Being relate to a tiny, inferior creature called man? At the start, we are told that they walked and talked in the garden. But God's enemy, Satan, seduced God's children. Tempted by Satan, they disobeyed God and hid from His presence. God expelled them from the beautiful home He had created for them.

King David speaks of this wonder: "When I consider Thy heavens, the work of Thy fingers, the moon and the stars, which Thou hast ordained; what is man, that Thou dost take thought of him? And the son of man that Thou dost care for him? Yet Thou hast made him a little lower than God, and dost crown him with glory and majesty" (Psalm 7:3–5). Most people ignored God. Some were obedient and tried to obey Him, but mankind was stubborn and disobedient. How could they ever be perfect, so they could again fellowship with their heavenly Father?

The Father strove through the centuries with the coming and going of civilizations, always reaching out to His wayward creatures. He did this in every possible way but especially through prophets and teachers. How could sinful men know perfect God? There had to be a way that men and women could know God in a personal way. Man was not able to accomplish this on his own. His finite mind could not comprehend the infinite.

God's solution was to become man and dwell among His people. He would walk with them and talk to them. He would be God and man all at the same time.

Then the nature of God would be clear to all. People on Earth could see what God was like. They could behold His perfect love and faithfulness. The Creator of the Earth came to His creation through a doorway called Bethlehem. Because of His coming, the world would never again be the same.

"And the Word became flesh, and dwelt among us, and we beheld His glory, glory as of the only begotten from the Father, full of grace and truth" (John 1:14).

"God, after He spoke long ago to the fathers in the prophets in many portions and in many ways, in these last days has spoken to us in His Son, whom He appointed heir of all things, through whom also He made the world. And He is the radiance of His glory and the exact representation of His nature, and upholds all things by the word of His power. When he had made purification of sins, He sat down at the right hand of the Majesty on high" (Hebrews 1:1–3).

Now man had a way to know God in a personal way. Jesus made that *way* through His sacrifice on the cross. Our responsibility and opportunity is to help unsaved people find that *way*.

Notes

GOD THE FATHER

Fathers who are mean and who do not spend high-quality time with their children corrupt the image that children have of the concept of father. When these children hear about God the Father, they are prone to negative thoughts about the idea of a loving heavenly father. Fathers who are like what God wants them to be make it easier for their children to accept the reality of a heavenly Father and are much more likely to believe in Him.

"Fathers, do not provoke your children to anger, but bring them up in the discipline and instruction of the Lord" (Ephesians 6:4). As fathers and to some extent grandfathers, we have the obligation and opportunity to help our children and grandchildren come to love and trust their heavenly Father. What is our heavenly Father like?

I get this statement from *The Baptist Faith and Message,* by Hobbs.[14]

> In the Bible God is seen as reigning in providential care over His creation and His creatures. He directs the flow of human history according to His redemptive purpose. This is evidenced in His choice of Abraham and his descendants, the nation of Israel and that nation's relationship to other nations.
>
> Thus one sees within history, God's holy history, wherein he directs the affairs of men and nations toward the fulfillment of His redemptive purpose. As Father, God is infinite in love, power, knowledge and wisdom. As Father, God cares for all of His creation. The clear revelation of God as Father came through Jesus. This is seen in John 20:17. "I ascend unto my Father and your Father; and to my God, and your God." Jesus is God's Son. Men become sons of God through faith in Jesus Christ.
>
> The universal fatherhood of God is a beautiful ideal, but it is not a reality. All men are God's creatures, but as such are not God's children. God is fatherly in His attitude toward everyone. He wills that *every person* shall be *His child.* But He is Father in truth only to those who become His children through faith in His Son.

Here is the best-known verse in the Bible: "God so loved the world that He gave His only begotten Son, that whoever believes in Him should not perish, but have eternal life" (John 3:16).

This passage pretty much says it all: "Blessed be the God and Father of our Lord Jesus Christ, who has blessed us with every spiritual blessing in the heavenly places in Christ: just as He chose us in Him before the foundation of the world, that we should be holy and blameless before Him. In love He predestined us to adoption as sons through Jesus Christ to Himself, according to the kind intention of His will, to the praise of the glory of His grace, which He freely bestowed on us in the Beloved. In Him we have redemption through His blood, the forgiveness of our trespasses, according to the riches of His grace, which He lavished on us. In all wisdom and insight He made known to us the mystery of His will, according to His kind intention which He purposed in Him with a view to an administration suitable to the fullness of the times, that is, the summing up of all things in Christ, things in the heavens, and things upon the earth" (Ephesians 1:3–10).

What a privilege it is to be a child in the family of God the Father! May God help us to be His obedient and grateful children!

Notes

The Trinity

The word *Trinity* does not appear in the Bible, but God is revealed in Scripture as three distinct persons. He is one and yet three. We have already considered God as Father. As God the Father, He is invisible; men could not see Him. The most mentioned of His attributes is holiness. "Let them praise Thy great and awesome name; Holy is He" (Psalm 99:3). "And one called out to another and said, 'Holy, Holy, Holy is the Lord of hosts, the whole earth is full of His glory" (Isaiah 6:3). God the Father is totally separate and apart from any other entity in the universe.

The second person of the Trinity is the Son. The four gospels present God the Son living with humans. Jesus enabled us to see God. He said, "He who has seen Me has seen the Father; how do you say, 'Show us the Father'?" (John 14:9b). If we want to know what God is like, look to Jesus. As Jesus, God became visible and He came near. He came as a man as Jesus Christ and lived with humans and lived with them in person. "No man has seen God at any time; the only begotten God, who is in the bosom of the Father, He has explained Him" (John 1:18). In Jesus a key attribute of God is revealed. "God so loved the world that He gave His only begotten Son" (John 3:16a). God, who the psalmist referred to as great and terrible, now became a loving Father to those who called on Him. "And it shall be, that everyone who calls on the name of the Lord shall be saved" (Acts 2:21).

The Holy Spirit is the third member of the Trinity. He arrived spectacularly: "And suddenly there came from heaven a noise like a violent, rushing wind, and it filled the whole house where they were sitting. And there appeared to them tongues as of fire distributing themselves, and they rested on each one of them. And they were all filled with the Holy Spirit" (Acts 2:3–4a). He came to the believers who were in one place in the upper room, just as Jesus had promised: "And I will ask the Father, and He will give you another Helper that He may be with you forever; that is the Spirit of truth, who the world cannot receive because it does not behold Him or know Him, but you know Him because He abides with you and will be in you" (John 14:16–17).

Although God is three persons, He is, at the same time, one. "Hear, O Israel! The Lord is our God, The Lord is one! And you shall love the Lord your God with all your heart and with all your soul and with all your might" (Deuteronomy 6:4–5). We can only speculate how three can be one. They each seem to have a different function, but in spirit and in purpose, as they relate to mankind, they are one.

All three members of the Trinity are included in several other Scriptures: "But the Helper, the Holy Spirit, whom the Father will send in My name, He will teach you all things, and bring to your remembrance all that I said to you" (John 14:26). In the Great Commission, Jesus said, "Go therefore and make disciples of all the nations, baptizing them in the name of the Father and the Son and the Holy Spirit" (Matthew 28:19). In Hebrews it says, "How much more will the blood of Christ, who through the eternal Spirit offered Himself without blemish to God, cleanse your conscience from dead works to serve the living God" (Hebrews 9:14). A beautiful hymn reminds us there is a Trinity.

> Holy, Holy, Holy Lord God almighty[15]
> Early in the morning, our song shall rise to Thee;
> Holy, Holy, Holy, merciful and mighty,
> God in three Persons blessed Trinity.

Notes

THE BIBLE

Baptists have been called a people of the Book. We base doctrine, church policy, and practice and guidelines for living on the sixty-six books in the Bible. The Bible we believe in was written by more than fifty writers who were as different as kings and fishermen. They wrote in places as varied as palaces and prisons. They wrote over a period of 1,500 years. They were from different countries and wrote in several different languages. The Bible was written in a variety of literary styles, including poetry, prose, and prophecies.

A reader who didn't know how the Bible was written might conclude that it was written by one person. We know, of course, that it was written under divine inspiration. The writers, in a sense, wrote over their heads. They put together words that meant more than they knew. David in Psalm 22 wrote, "They pierced my hands and my feet," and Isaiah in chapter 53 wrote, "He was pierced through for our transgressions." They wrote more about Calvary than they realized. Not only was it written under God's supervision, but it was preserved by God. There have been attempts to destroy it.

Men have been executed for preaching it, and yet it remains the best seller of all time. Voltaire stood in Paris more than 250 years ago and said that although it took twelve men to originate the Christian religion, it would take only one to eliminate it. Then he dipped his pen into the ink of hatred of his heart and wrote against God's book and Christianity. Voltaire is no more but Christianity thrives. On the very spot where he uttered these words, there is a printing press operated by a Bible Society that sends Bibles to every nation on Earth.

Imagine an author writing today and fifty others writing over the next 1,500 years, and without consulting with one another, there comes from their writings a book that seems to have been written by one person. Moses, who wrote Exodus, didn't confer with John, who wrote Revelation, and yet they and all the books in between allude to one who would come or has come to save man from his sin.

One of the great miracles of the Bible is that though no original manuscripts exist, the Bible we read today, when compared with old manuscripts that were discovered after the Bible was formed, is remarkably consistent and accurate. God has protected the message of salvation through all the many translations. The Bible continues to be our authority for religious and spiritual matters. It reveals God in

Christ reconciling the world to Himself. It is final for us in all matters of Christian faith and practice.

It is interesting to note that Psalm 118:8 is the middle verse in the Bible and tells us, "It is better to take refuge in the Lord than to trust in man."

Both Jesus and the Bible are both human and divine.

Wonderful Words of Life[16]
Sing them over again to me, Wonderful words of life
Let me more of their beauty see, Wonderful words of life
Words of life and beauty, teach me faith and duty:
Beautiful words, wonderful words, wonderful words of life
Beautiful words, wonderful words, wonderful words of life.

Notes

Spiritual Gifts

In his book *The Purpose Driven Life*[17] Rick Warren challenges Christians to find their spiritual gift and put it to work for the Lord. In his little book *Meditations on the Purpose Driven Life* he asks, "Why do I exist? Why am I here? What is my purpose?" Among his many statements he says, "We were shaped for serving God." Paul said, "For we are His workmanship, created in Christ Jesus unto good works" (Ephesians 2:10).

A good question to ask is, "What good works should I do?" Part of the answer lies in discovering and understanding our spiritual gift(s). First Corinthians 12 and 14 discuss these gifts. Chapter 13 is the love chapter. I think it is included here as a reminder that whatever our gift or type of service, it should be dominated and permeated by agape love, which is always doing that which is in the best interest of the other person. Verse 7 in chapter 12 reads, "But to each one of us is given the manifestation of the Spirit for the common good." Paul then lists some of the gifts: "wisdom, knowledge, faith, healing, miracles, prophesy, tongues, interpretation of tongues."

I heard of a pastor in California who spoke in tongues. He didn't know what he was saying until he found someone who could interpret tongues. The answer was "Get rid of your deacons." I think this was not an actual event but a joke.

Paul in, 1 Corinthians 14, has some more to say about tongues. In verse 28 he says, "Without someone to interpret, keep silent." In verse 19 he says, "I desire to speak five words with my mind, that I may instruct others also, rather than 10,000 words in a tongue." Romans 12 lists gifts starting in verse 6: prophecy, service, teaching, exhortation, liberality, leadership, and mercy. A good book on the subject is *19 Gifts of the Spirit*,[18] by Leslie Flynn.

Warren in his book challenges Christians to discover their gift and put it to work for the Lord. We need to be reminded that every one of us has at least one spiritual gift. I have heard it said that other people can tell what our gift is better than we can. I guess mine is administration, because starting when I was first saved, I ended up in charge of something no matter where I went. In California, shortly after I got out of the army, I was saved. I started going to the young adult Training Union at the Richmond Baptist Church. Before long, I was president of that union.

In Nashville, I was a member of Two Rivers Baptist Church, and became the first deacon chairman. I served in that capacity seven different times. For some thirty-five years I was the church library director. In no instance did I ask for any of these positions. Not too long after I became a member of Immanuel Baptist Church in Lexington, Kentucky, I ended up being Training Union director. After a few years there they asked me to be minister of education. Eight years later I ended up supervising the Field Services Section for the Library Department at the Sunday School Board. Don't think I'm boasting. It's just a way of sharing a bit of my life as an example of others recognizing a gift I didn't know I had. Actually, at the beginning, I had no idea there was such a thing as a spiritual gift.

My guess is there are many Christians who are not aware of their spiritual gift. What a loss it is to the life of our churches that so many spiritual gifts are lying dormant.

What is That in My Hand?[19]
What was in thy hand David?
Only a shepherd's sling;
But a mighty giant reeled and fell
When he gave the stone a fling.

Notes

Ministry

We need to be reminded from time to time of our obligations, responsibilities, and opportunities to minister to each other and to others in need. The following passage is a strong reminder of our obligation: "Blessed be the God and Father of our Lord Jesus Christ, the Father of mercies and God of all comfort; who comforts us in all of our afflictions so that we may be able to comfort those who are in any affliction with the comfort with which we ourselves are comforted by God" (2 Corinthian 1:3–4).

My church is organized so that Sunday school members are to minister to fellow members who are in need. Deacons are organized to minister to those who are not in Sunday school. Also, a deacon is assigned to each Sunday school department to guide leaders and members in their ministry. Organizing for ministry is vital to make sure that no one is missed.

Scripture reminds us of our responsibility: "And let us not lose heart in doing good, for in due time we shall reap if we do not grow weary. So then, while we have opportunity, let us do good to all men and especially to those who are of the household of faith" (Galatians 6:9–10). We shouldn't neglect people outside the church fellowship, but we are admonished to give special attention to fellow Christians. We are admonished to not tire of doing good. This recognizes the human tendency to give into the flesh instead of allowing the Spirit to control us.

John reminds us of who we are: "Beloved, let us love one another, for love is from God; and everyone who loves is born of God and knows God" (1 John 4–7). The way we treat each other is evidence that we know the Father.

Someone has said, "If you think growing up is hard, try growing old." Senior adults are those who have grown old, and any group of them anywhere could make a long list of bumps, bruises, broken bones, and disappointments. Of all the people in a church, senior adults should best understand their responsibility to care for each other. After the years of Bible study, Sunday school lessons, and sermons that most of them have experienced, they should know what God's will is for them and by experience have developed good ministry habits.

If someone is absent or hurting, it should be known and they should be missed and checked on. Even when a person is doing well, they can use a word of encouragement on a regular basis. It is interesting to note the use of the term *one another* in Scripture. For example, "For you were called to freedom, brethren; only do not turn your freedom into opportunity for the flesh, but through love serve *one another*" (Galatians 5:13). And, "That there should be no division in the body, but that the members should have the same care for *one another*" (1 Corinthians 12:25).

Ministering to each other in any group is not our only concern. We are to minister and care for people wherever we see the need. We need to keep in mind that one of our strongest influences on others is how they see us caring for each other. Our first concern for others is that they come to know and love Jesus Christ as Savior.

The love that Christians have for each other can serve as a magnet to draw the lost to the Savior.

Notes

WITNESSING

Every Christian bears a witness. A person's witness is either helpful or hurtful. The fact that every Christian is a witness means that we must be careful in all of our contacts and conduct to protect our reputation. It is a tragedy when a lost person uses misconduct on the part of a Christian as an excuse to reject Christ and His church. About sixty years ago, we had a study course at Immanuel Baptist Church in Lexington. It was based on C. E. Matthews's book, *Every Christian's Job*. It was through that experience that I concluded that living a good life and inviting people to church was not enough. A real witness must include the sharing of Christ with lost people. There are many different ways to share Christ. We need to work at finding a way that we are comfortable using.

James says, "My brethren, if any among you strays from the truth, and one turns him back, let him know that he who turns a sinner from the error of his way will save his soul from death and will cover a multitude of sins" (James 5:19–20). The apostle Paul said, "I have become all things to all men that I may by all means save some" (1 Corinthians 9:22). Becoming all things meant he would take whatever steps were necessary to relate to a lost person. Paul also said, "Brethren, my heart's desire and my prayer to God for them is for their salvation" (Roman 10:1). Paul was talking about his fellow Jews. This was an expression of concern for lost people.

We probably won't work at witnessing until we have developed a concern for the lost. This concern will develop to the extent that we believe the lost will spend an eternity in hell. Also, we know the joy of salvation and should hope that those who are lost will come to have that same joy.

Some people are turned away by a hard-sell witness. It is important that we sense when someone is under conviction and ready to listen—and think like Paul, who said "by all means." There are many ways to share the gospel. Jim's testimony went something like this: A neighbor backed him into a corner and tried to compel him to trust Christ. Another friend brought him some books. One of the books was *The Goal and the Glory* by Ted Simonson. This book contained the Christian testimony of some well-known professional athletes—some of the same athletes that Jim watched on television. Placing this book in Jim's hands enabled these Christian athletes to witness to Jim. It would have been better if one of them could have actually visited Jim, but the book was the next best thing.

Sharing books and tracts is one means of winning people to Christ. Paul said "by all means." Chuck Colson was won to Christ when a congressman gave him a copy of C. S. Lewis's book *Mere Christianity*.

We are told in the book of Acts, "You shall receive power when the Holy Spirit has come upon you; and you shall be my witnesses in Jerusalem, and in all Judea and Samaria, and even to the remotest part of the earth" (Acts 1:8). You shall be! To be is what we are, and what we are is a *witness* to our Lord Jesus Christ. And, we are promised power. We are not on our own. We are not alone when we seek to help someone see their need of a savior.

Witness While You Can

While you are well and in control,
Give Christ the use of your mind, heart and soul.
Working together with Him,
Some will be saved from a life of sin.

Notes

Baptism and the Lord's Supper

Baptism and the Lord's Supper are called ordinances because they are decrees or commands. They are not sacraments, because they do not have saving power. Both are symbols and are performed as acts of obedience. When done correctly, they serve to proclaim the essential elements of the gospel message, namely the death, burial, and resurrection of our Lord Jesus and the birth to new life of the baptismal candidate. Romans gives the best description or meaning of baptism. "Therefore we have been buried with Him through baptism into death in order that as Christ was raised from the dead through the glory of the Father, so we too might walk in newness of life" (Romans 6:4).

Baptism is an act of obedience by one already saved. It is a testimony of what has already been accomplished. It is a public profession of faith. If the audience is told that baptism is part of salvation, baptism communicates error and is invalid. If the candidate is unsaved, baptism is meaningless. Two pictures are involved in baptism. For the candidate it portrays the burial of the old life and the rising to a new life in Christ. The baptism also serves to remind the audience of the burial and resurrection of our Lord Jesus.

The Lord's Supper is best described in 1 Corinthians 11:23–34. In verse 24, Jesus says, "This [the bread] is my body, which is for you; do this in remembrance of me," and in verse 25 concerning the cup, "This cup is the new covenant in my blood; do this as often as you drink it, in remembrance of Me." The Lord's Supper serves to remind us of our Lord's sacrificial death on the cross.

As long as these two ordinances are observed correctly, they picture accurately the gospel message that Christ died, shed His blood, was buried, and on the third day was resurrected. The audience is made to understand that the baptismal candidate has placed his faith in the risen Christ and is a new person in Him.

It is important that people, especially new Christians, understand the meaning of the two ordinances and that they are performed true to the Scriptures. An elderly lady, a longtime member of a Southern Baptist church, came forward in a service requesting baptism. Her husband was a deacon. Years before she had joined a Northern Baptist church by letter or statement from a church that baptized by sprinkling. Her new church either received such people or didn't ask about her baptism. She had joined the Southern Baptist church by letter, and that church didn't ask her about her baptism, just assuming that since she came from a Baptist church, she had been baptized by immersion. She had been troubled for many years that she had come to that church improperly. This lady had been troubled, or felt guilty, for many years, because deep down, she knew that her baptism was not scriptural.

I am sensitive to this because before going overseas, in World War II, I went forward at the Immanuel Baptist Church in Lexington, Kentucky. They had a special morning baptismal service for me. No one questioned me or explained anything to me. In my mind what I had done was a good thing that would go down on the right side of the books in heaven.

After I was out of the army I joined a group of dedicated young adults in a church in California. They involved me in Bible study. It wasn't long until I realized I wasn't saved, and I trusted Jesus with all the understanding and change in my life that made it real.

On my next time back to Lexington, I went forward and was properly baptized. I think if someone had asked some questions, it would have been apparent that I didn't understand what I was doing and it is quite possible I could have been led to a real conversion experience. I would have gone overseas a saved soldier. It is important to know what we believe not only for our own sake, but for the sake of others whom we have the opportunity to influence for the Lord.

It is good for us to believe alike about major Bible doctrines. The Bible speaks to this: "Now the God who gives perseverance and encouragement grant you to be of the same mind with one another, according to Christ Jesus; that with one accord you may with one voice glorify the God and Father of our Lord Jesus Christ" (Romans 15:5–6).

Notes

PRAYER

Without prayer, the Christian life would be like a ship without power or a rudder. In the Bible, prayer is a major subject. The various forms of the words *prayer* and *praise* appear in the Bible some 630 times.

"Pray without ceasing; in everything give thanks; for this is God's will for you in Christ Jesus" (1 Thessalonians 5:17–18). Paul said "in everything," not "for everything."   "Be anxious for nothing, but in everything by prayer and supplication with thanksgiving let your requests be made known to God" (Philippians 4:6). Instead of worrying, *pray*! We are not to leave out any part of life. Through prayer, we can involve God in everything.

Be alert by praying: "With all prayer and petition pray *at all times* in the Spirit, and with this in view, be on the alert with all perseverance and petition for all the saints" (Ephesians 6:18). Not just "pray about everything" but "at all times." Not just when we get up in the morning or when we go to bed at night, but at all times. Jesus said in Matthew 21:22, "And everything you ask in prayer, believing, you shall receive."

In all four gospels, the word *prayer* appears only nine times, and none of these is in the book of John. Three of these are where Jesus said, "My house shall be called a house of prayer." The model prayer in Luke 11:1–4 begins with "Lord teach us to pray just as John taught his disciples." (This refers to John the Baptist.) The passages in Luke and Matthew include praising the Father, and pleas for human needs such as daily bread, pardon for sins, and help to avoid temptation.

Some guidelines for prayer include abiding in Christ, praying according to His will, and praying in His name. James 4:3 says, "You ask and do not receive because you ask with wrong motives, so that you may spend it on your pleasures." The reason we pray is as important as the prayer itself. We shouldn't pray to be seen doing so, and we should avoid endless repetitions.

Finally, when we don't know what to pray for, the Holy Spirit helps us. "In the same way the Spirit also helps our weakness; for we do not know how to pray as we should, but the Spirit Himself intercedes for us with groanings too deep for words; and He who searches the hearts knows what the mind of the Spirit is, because He intercedes for the saints according to the will of God" (Romans 8:26–27).

Many years ago, my first wife led an adult group in a study of prayer. This study went on every Sunday evening for four months. The concept of prayer is an immense subject. At the end of the study, the group discovered that the Holy Spirit helps us know what to pray for. Perhaps, out of the clear blue, you have had someone's name come to mind. Isn't it possible that the person needed help and the Holy Spirit was prompting you to pray?

Brother Lawrence wrote a little book titled *The Practice of the Presence of God*. That sounds a whole lot like "pray without ceasing." Being aware of who we are in Christ is not just for when we are at church in a worship service. We need to be aware of Christ when we are at work, at play, and shopping at the mall. He has promised never to leave us or forsake us. We are reminded of this in Hebrews 13:5b: "I will never desert you, nor will I ever forsake you." Prayer is the way we stay connected with this promise.

Notes

The Church

The New Testament church is a local body of baptized believers in the Lord Jesus Christ. The church is the body of Christ with Him as the head. The church is also the bride of Christ with him as the groom. The church as bride and body refers to all the saved of all time. It is good to know that we are included in that great host, but it important that we be a part of the local body where worship and work takes place.

Jesus said, "I will build my church" (Matthew 16:18). Paul said, "To the church of God which is at Corinth, to those who have been sanctified in Christ Jesus, saints by calling, with all who in every place call upon the name of our Lord Jesus Christ" (1 Corinthians 1:2).

It is interesting to note that the word *saint* appears seven times before Acts 21:16 and fifty-seven times in the twenty-two books after Acts. The word *disciple* is not used after Acts 21:16. A saint is one "set apart." One possible explanation is that *disciple* was used for those who followed Jesus while He was on earth, and *saints* made up the membership of the newly formed churches. A saint is one set apart. This could mean that Christians are saints, set apart to work with Christ in building His church.

Churches were given marching orders: "You shall receive power when the Holy Spirit has come upon you; and you shall be my witnesses both in Jerusalem, and in all Judea and Samaria, and even to the remotest part of the earth" (Acts 1:8). The disciples were assembled in the upper room when this promise was fulfilled: "And suddenly there came from heaven a noise like a violent, rushing wind, and it filled the whole house where they were sitting. And there appeared to them tongues as of fire distributing themselves, and they rested on each one. And they were all filled with the Holy Spirit and began to speak with other tongues, as the Spirit was giving them utterance" (Acts 2:2-4). People in Jerusalem who spoke many languages were able to hear the gospel in their own tongue. Many were saved, and this gave the fledging church a real boost.

Next came persecution of Christians, and this caused them to scatter, finally leading to the formation of a church at Antioch. Gentiles were being saved, and they were first called Christians at Antioch. Saints are challenged: "Let us hold fast the confession of our hope without wavering, for He who promised is faithful, and let us consider how to stimulate one another to love and good deeds not forsaking our own assembling together as is the habit of some, but encouraging one another, and all the more as you see the day drawing near" (Hebrews (10:23–24).

Churches now circle the globe, but there are yet multitudes without the Savior and vast areas without a church. While we enjoy each other within our own church, we must continue to reach out through giving, praying, and going.

Jesus said to Peter, "I will build My church; and the gates of Hades shall not over power it" (Matthew 16:18b). Jesus is still at work building His church. We are partners with Him when we work to strengthen *His* church, of which we are members, and as we support missions through our giving and praying.

Notes

STEWARDSHIP

According to the Bible a steward is someone who is responsible for something that belongs to another. God *owns* everything: "For every beast of the forest is Mine, the cattle on a thousand hills. I know every bird of the mountains, and everything that moves in the field is Mine. If I were hungry, I would not tell you; for the world is Mine, and all it contains" (Psalm 50:10–12). God made everything, and He has not released His claim. He created man to take care of His handiwork for Him.

"What do you have that you did not receive?" (1 Corinthians 4:7). We work, earn money, and buy property. The deed at the courthouse has our name on it as the owner. God made the land and all the material that went into the house, and He has never relinquished ownership.

First Corinthians 4:2 reminds us that "moreover it is required of stewards that a man be found trustworthy." The following statement comes from *The Baptist Faith and Message*[20] by Herschel Hobbs:

> God is the source of all blessings, temporal and spiritual; all that we have and are we owe to Him. Christians have a holy trusteeship in the gospel, and a binding stewardship in their possessions. They are therefore under obligation to serve Him with their time, talents, and material possessions; and should recognize all these as entrusted to them to use for the glory of God and for helping others. According to the Scriptures, Christians should contribute of their means cheerfully, regularly, systematically, proportionately, and liberally for the advancement of the Redeemer's cause on earth.

Some people say that the New Testament doesn't teach tithing. It may teach that we should give more than the tithe. Jesus in Matthew 23:23 commended the Pharisees for tithing. I heard a sermon once in which the preacher called attention to the fact that our Savior is a "Priest forever according to the order of Melchizedek" (Hebrew 7:17). All we know about Melchizedek is that he was king of Salem, he had neither beginning nor ending of life, and he received tithes from Abraham. Jesus should be receiving our tithe!

According to Jesus' comment about the widow's mite, He measures the gift by the love and sacrifice it involves. Attitude toward giving is important to God. First Corinthians 9:7 tells us that "God loves a cheerful giver." I remember a preacher saying that that word *cheerful* could be translated as "hilarious." In Philippians 4:15–18 Paul tells how the Philippians had been sacrificial and faithful in giving to his needs. Then in verse 19 he said, "My God shall supply all your needs according to His riches in glory in Christ Jesus." We take the nineteenth verse out of context when we generalize it.

These verses sound a lot like Matthew 6:31–33: "Do not be anxious then, saying, 'What shall we eat? Or 'What shall we drink?' or 'With what shall we clothe ourselves?' For all these things the Gentiles eagerly seek; for your heavenly Father knows that you need all these things. But seek first His kingdom and His righteousness and all these things shall be added to you." God owns us and loves us. He is a responsible Father who takes care of His children.

We are all familiar with Malachi 3:10: "'Bring the whole tithe into the storehouse, so that there may be food in My house, and test Me now in this,' says the Lord of hosts, 'if I will not open for you the windows of heaven, and pour out for you a blessing until there is no more need.'"

Many Christians eagerly receive the promises in Psalm 23 while at the same time rejecting the requirement of Malachi 3:10.

Notes

CREATION

Many years ago I debated with myself about how we came to be. Did God make us fully formed, or did he make the stuff of which we are made and turn that stuff loose to fend for itself until life somehow came out of the muck or whatever you might call the stuff? There is much speculation how it might have happened, such as lightning striking the goo and the winds and the waves constantly churning the mix until patterns developed and some form of life came to be. For those who don't believe in God there is the problem of accounting for where everything came from in the first place.

Then there is the problem of the second law of thermodynamics, which says that when matter is mixed, like in a mixing bowl, everything homogenizes rather than developing patterns. We and all of life are complex patterns. I stopped speculating after reading Dr. W. A. Criswell's book, *Did Man Just Happen?* I decided that since there was no scientific proof that evolution could produce life, I didn't need to waste my time thinking about it. The Bible simply says in Genesis 1:1, "In the beginning God created the heavens and the earth."

The Bible says: "In the beginning was the Word, and the Word was with God, and the Word was God. He was in the beginning with God. All things came into being by Him; and apart from Him nothing came into being that has come into being" (John 1:1–3).

The Bible says, "Worthy art thou our Lord and our God, to receive glory and honor and power, for Thou didst create all things, because of Thy will they existed and were created" (Revelation 4:11).

The Bible tells us that man has no excuse for not believing in God, "For since the creation of the world His invisible attributes, His eternal power and divine nature, have been clearly seen, being understood through what has been made, so that they are without excuse" (Romans 1:20). I look at all the beauty around us—and no place is more beautiful than the Smoky Mountains in the fall—and ask, "Who or what can appreciate such beauty other than man?" God gave us the senses that we use to see, feel, and hear the glories of His creation. The things we can see with the microscope and the telescope are even more amazing.

I have heard it said that if all the space were removed between the electrons, protons, and neutrons that make up the atom, Earth would be the size of a basketball.

Robert Gange tells us in his book *Origins and Destiny*[21] that red blood cells are made up of 270 million hemoglobin molecules, each with 574 amino acids of 21 different types. It was said that if one of those amino acids was missing or out of place, you had sickle cell anemia. This all amounted to 155 billion amino acid entities in each of 33 trillion red blood cells. This describes how really complex we are.

In *Creation's Tiny Mystery*[22] by Robert Gentry, the author tells about polonium halos in granite. Gentry sliced granite into very thin pieces, so thin that light would shine through. What he found were halo patterns. Geologists say that it took four and a half billion years for granite to form. Gentry's halos prove that if it had taken more than three and a half minutes for granite to harden, there would have been no halo patterns.

Scientists have a Colossian theory: "And He is before all things and in Him all things hold together" (Colossians 1:27). In atoms there are protons, which have a positive charge. Positive charges are supposed to repel, but in atoms they attract. When an atom is split, that attraction energy is released, if that power ceased for a moment, there would be no forms in the entire universe.

David thanked the Lord for being "fearfully and wonderfully made" (Psalm 139:14). Even without all this scientific knowledge, David realized we were *made* and not an accident of nature.

Notes

The Ten Commandments

The Ten

Someone has said, "These are ten commandments, not ten suggestions." Here are the ten in abbreviated form (using the Holman Christian Standard Bible, (Exodus 20:3–17) :

1. Do not have other gods besides Me.
2. Do not make an idol for yourself.
3. Do not misuse the name of the Lord your God
4. Remember the Sabbath day, to keep it holy.
5. Honor your father and your mother.
6. Do not murder.
7. Do not commit adultery.
8. Do not steal.
9. Do not give false testimony against your neighbor.
10. Do not covet anything that belongs to your neighbor.

The first four commandments deal with man's relationship to God. The other six relate to our relationship with each other. God gave us these moral laws. They are as valid today as they were the day Moses came down off the mountains with the tablets.

Without these laws we would not have civilization as we know it. The laws are the basis of civilized life. They are eternal truth. There is no way to exaggerate the importance of the commandments. Without them, men would very likely destroy each other.

The commandments came to mankind while Moses was leading the children of Israel out of Egypt. The exodus is a picture of man's leaving the bondage of sin into the freedom we enjoy in Christ. Even Christians need to be reminded of the rules that help us live together in peace. Israel was getting out of slavery in Egypt. Moses received the commandments from God while on the mountain. There is more to each of these commandments than many people realize. The next ten devotionals will deal with each one in detail.

Jesus said, "Don't assume that I came to destroy the Law or the Prophets. I did not come to destroy, but to fulfill. For I assure you: Until heaven and earth pass away, not the smallest letter or one stroke of a letter will pass from the law until all things are accomplished" (Matthew 5:17–18, HCSB).

The law is strict, but we have the Holy Spirit to guide us and convict us when slip. "No, in all these things we are more than victorious through Him who loved us" (Romans 8:37, HCSB).

The law is still in effect. Some people may think keeping the law will save them. We know that there is no way anyone can avoid breaking the law. God sent Jesus, who was able to keep the law. He committed no sin. He then was able to be the sacrifice for sin, and God sees His sinless life and gives it to us when we trust Christ for salvation.

The law is used to help unsaved people know they are sinners. "Wherefore the law was our schoolmaster, to bring us unto Christ, that we might be justified by faith" (Galatians 3:24, KJV). The commandments are still working to help mankind know God's will, to help us know right from wrong, and to help bring us to the Savior.

Notes

No Other Gods

"Do not have other gods besides Me" (Exodus 20:3, HCSB) and (Deuteronomy 5:7, HCSB). The word *God* is in the Bible more than 4.330 times, almost four times per page. God is a major subject in Scripture.

Just think about this passage: "For God's wrath is revealed from heaven against all godlessness and unrighteousness of people, who by their unrighteousness suppress the truth, since what can be known about God is evident among them, because God has shown it to them. For His invisible attributes, that is, His eternal power and divine nature have been clearly seen since the creation of the world, being understood through what He has made. As a result, people are without excuse" (Romans 1:18–20, HCSB).

Who can observe the beauties and complexities of nature and not conclude that there is a Creator? Speaking of complexities, people in Paul's day had no idea how complex life really is. They didn't have the electron microscope that enabled men to see the complex cells of living tissue. How much more are people without excuse who know what we now know about God's creation?

Because of what we now know about nature and life, this passage could be stated even more strongly than was said by the psalmist: "The fool says in his heart, 'God does not exist'" (Psalm 14:1 and 53:1, HCSB). Based on this definition of a fool, there are many fools in the world today.

The Bible begins with "In the beginning God created the heavens and the earth" (Genesis 1:1). Before this first verse, nothing existed but God, the Trinity, and the angels. Because of the long life of humans before the flood, the first people would have heard from their grandfather, Adam, how God walked with him and Eve in the garden.

J. B. Philips authored a book titled *Your God Is Too Small.* Man's limited concept of God prevents him from trusting Him like he could and should. According to Matthew 14:31, HCSB, here is what Jesus said to Peter when a little wind and rain caused him to doubt Jesus: "O you of little faith, why did you doubt?" Peter's concept of Jesus was too small and caused him to fear. God today is the God of Exodus: "I am the Lord your God,

He is the same God who saved us from the bondage of sin. "For God loved the world in this way: He gave His One and only Son, so that everyone who believes in Him will have eternal life" (John 3:16, HCSB).

I was witnessing to my ninety-two-year-old uncle. He didn't accept Christ on that occasion, but he did say he could still hear his mother, my grandmother Effie Mee, singing as she went about her work in the kitchen, "And He walks with me and He talks with me and he tells me I am His own and the joys we share as we tarry there none other has ever known."[23] My grandmother, though gone for many years, was still bearing witness to her Savior and God. May we do likewise as we go, wherever we go.

Notes

MAKE NO IDOLS

"Do not make an idol for yourself, whether in the shape of anything in the earth. You must not bow down to them or worship them; for I, the Lord your God, am a jealous God, punishing the children for the father's sin, to the third and fourth generations of those who hate Me, but showing faithful love to a thousand generations of those who love Me and keep My commands" (Exodus 20:4–6, HCSB).

People in the nations near the children of Israel worshipped many false gods. There was a genuine danger that God's people would take up the practices of these neighbors. Primitive peoples today can be found making idols from wood or picking up oddly shaped rocks. They bow down to these false gods. We think of such as superstition. When fear strikes, they will cling to something they have made or found. This then becomes an object of worship.

Moses told his people to avoid that. Today we may think this commandment doesn't apply to us. We know that sticks and stones of whatever shape and size have no power to help us. Nothing of that sort deserves our adoration or worship. We deny it, but there probably are some things in our life that we admire too much. We may not bow down to them the way we worship God, but we may have an emotional attachment to the thing, and give it so much time that it is almost like worship. It may actually crowd God out of our life or give Him very little of our time and attention.

When we give time and attention to something that crowds God out, it is similar to worshiping an idol. We could get defensive and say, "We don't carve an object and bow down to it." But there is a concept in this commandment that says that anything that takes the place God should have in our life becomes an idol. The idea of God's jealousy is not the same as people's jealousy. It means that God must be first in one's life. He will not be relegated to second place while we allow something else to dominate us.

What about visiting the iniquity of the fathers on the children? Each person is accountable to God. "The person who sins is the one who will die" (Ezekiel 18:20, HCSB). God does not punish the son for the father's sin, but it is true in many cases that the child sins because of the bad influence of the father. In many cases the children suffer because of the father's neglect.

We need to read and live by Matthew 22:37–40, HCSB: "Love the Lord your God with all your heart, and with all your soul, and with your entire mind. This is the greatest and most important commandment. The second is like it: Love your neighbor as yourself. All the Law and the Prophets depend on these two commandments."

If we abide by this admonition, we will not be guilty of worshipping an idol or neglecting God in any way.

Notes

You Shall Not Abuse God's Name

"Do not misuse the name of the Lord your God, because the Lord will punish anyone who misuses His name" (Exodus 20:7, HCSB). In the Bible, names have meaning. They describe the nature of the person and his purpose. Because names mean something, they are more than just a way to address a person and thus demand more respect. Respect for God shows up in the way we use His name. The ancient Jews were so conscious of this that they wouldn't utter His name at all.

Misuse means using the name for purposes other than addressing the person. The prohibition can include not using His name as an "open sesame." The commandment prohibits the thoughtless use of God's name in prayers. Some people use a slang word that is a derivation of God's name. We are not to include the Lord's name in everyday conversation. For some this is just a careless habit. Such use shows disrespect for the name and is prohibited by this commandment. We are not to use our Lord's name in any way that is not sincere or an honor to Him.

Scripture says, "But let your statement be, 'yes, yes' or 'no, no'; and anything beyond these is evil" (Matthew 5:37). Let your yes be yes and your no be no, without the addition of the Deity. Sometimes we want to make sure the people we are speaking to understand we really mean what we are saying, so we "underline" it with graphic words. Such speech is way beyond just saying yes or no.

We need to be very thoughtful about our pledges or oaths with respect to giving or service. I once made a commitment to witness to at least one person every day. I failed to think it through and found it was very difficult to find at least one person I could witness to or that I was too busy to even think about it.

"Again, you have heard that it was said to our ancestors, **"You must not break your oath, but you must keep your oaths to the Lord**. But I tell you, don't take an oath at all: either by heaven, because it is God's throne; or by the earth, because it is His footstool; or by Jerusalem, because it is the city of the great King. Neither should you swear by your head, because you cannot make a single hair white or black. But let your word 'yes' be 'yes,' and your 'no' be 'no.' Anything more than this is from the evil one" (Matthew 5:33–37, HCSB).

We may think that our use of a word that is a substitute for God or Jesus is harmless, but it is really a careless or disrespectful attitude toward

God. This is especially harmful because it is a blotch on our testimony and harmful to our influence on those around us. We may oversimplify this commandment by thinking it is a prohibition against the use of God's name in profanity, but it is much more than that.

Before I was saved, when I was in the army, I developed a really bad habit of using vulgar words and God's name in my speech. One day, after I was out of the army, I was driving, with my mother beside me, and another car cut too close in front of us. I called out the window to the driver, using a very vulgar expression. In that moment God convicted me of how really sinful I was. He got my attention, and shortly afterward I confessed my sin and received Christ. My bad habit was corrected, and to this day I have not uttered another word of profanity.

I believe the sin that causes a person to come under conviction gets corrected in the salvation experience.

We cannot expect anyone around us to respect our testimony if we are careless and disrespectful in our use of God's name in any of its forms.

Notes

Remember the Sabbath Day to Keep It Holy

"Remember to dedicate the Sabbath day: You are to labor six days and do all your work, but the seventh day is a Sabbath to the Lord your God. You must not do any work—you, your son or daughter, your male or female slave, your livestock, or the foreigner who is within your gates. For the Lord made the heavens and the earth, the sea, and everything in them in six days; then He rested on the seventh day. Therefore the Lord blessed the Sabbath day and declared it holy" (Exodus 20:8–11, HCSB).

We are reminded of much in these few verses. We doubt that God required rest, but perhaps He rested to set an example for His creation, which would need rest. His creation would require not only rest but time to reflect on the One who made them and everything that existed. Included in the commandment is the requirement that owners of animals and servants were not to take advantage of them by overworking them. They needed rest as well as the owner.

Perhaps some of the developments in modern society came about in part because of this commandment. The inclusion of slaves and servants in the commandment meets a real need and puts the responsibility on the ones in power to do something about it.

One of my ancestors supposedly worked in the French linen mills at age four. This was in the 1800s. The forty-hour workweek, minimum-wage laws, and child labor laws could all have their origin in the sentiment of this commandment.

The main thrust of the commandment has to do with honoring the Sabbath, to keep it holy, or set apart. Contained in the commandment is the phrase *a Sabbath to the Lord your God.* Observing the Lord's Day can prevent work and weariness from causing us to forget the Lord and all He has done and is doing. The Sabbath gives us a time for worship and reflection on the Lord's goodness and provision. We choose to observe the Sabbath. Exercising our free will and giving our time to obey the Lord's command is part of our worship.

The Jewish leaders had corrupted the meaning of the Sabbath with hundreds of restrictions. Jesus said the Sabbath was made for man and not man for the Sabbath. By healing a man with a withered hand and allowing his disciples to pluck grain for food on the Sabbath, Jesus gave a different meaning to the Sabbath. It meant that meeting the needs of humans was more important than rules.

There is the saying "Give a man an inch and he'll take a mile." We have doubtless gone way beyond meeting human needs to completely corrupting the Sabbath. Since Jesus visited His creation, in the flesh, it has been called the Lord's Day. With so many activities that are anything but rest and remembering the Lord, it could be called *our day*.

Notes

Honor Your Parents

"Honor your father and your mother so you may have a long life in the land that the LORD your God is giving you" (Exodus 20:12, HCSB). Deuteronomy adds "so that you may prosper" (5:16, HCSB). My mother died in 1967 and my father in 1981. They were honest, hardworking parents who were easy to respect. I am a parent, a grandparent, and a great-grandparent. God has blessed me with a second wife who is the same "grand." Between us we have twenty-six grandchildren and six great-grandchildren. We are truly honored by all of our children.

Admonition in Scripture to honor parents serves to remind us and condition us to respect and honor our heavenly Father. Parents who don't provide for their children, cannot be trusted, and mistreat their offspring make it very difficult for their children to trust their Father who is in heaven. In their minds, the vision of "father" is negative.

I think this is what is involved in Ephesians 5:22–6:3. This is where wives are told to submit to their own husbands as to the Lord and husbands are told to love their wives. Paul says, "I am speaking with reference to Christ and the church." I take this to mean that in an ideal home the husband is the head of the family as Christ is head of the church. The wife represents the church and is loved by her husband as Christ loves His bride the church.

Paul goes on to say, "CHILDREN, obey your parents in the Lord, for this is right. HONOR YOUR FATHER AND MOTHER, (which is the first commandment with a promise), THAT IT MAY BE WELL WITH YOU, AND THAT YOU MAY LIVE LONG ON THE EARTH" (Ephesians 6: 1– 3). We need to be reminded that God is our heavenly Father and that all who are saved are His children. In a sense we are one large interrelated family. If parents understand that the way they treat their children has eternal implications, they will more likely be parents who are easy to honor. Their children will be more likely to honor them. Those children who have a proper example of a father are much more likely to trust their heavenly Father. What a disaster it is when children's image of a father is corrupted by a mean, unloving father.

A proper understanding of Ephesians 5:22–6:3 might help parents realize that there is more involved than just the husband-wife relationship. There is a heavenly Father who loves them and to whom they are accountable. If parents understood that, the result would be more parents who deserve to be honored and more children who would come to trust Jesus Christ as Savior. This, after all, is the overriding objective in this life.

The home where the father is a loving leader and the mother and father together are the kind that children respect, trust, and obey is going to be a happy home. It will be a home that is a "good seed bed" out of which will sprout people who love the Lord and serve Him.

Notes

Do Not Murder

The sixth commandment is "Do not murder" (Exodus 20:13, HCSB). This commandment applies to a person—to an individual—not to a government. Some form of the words *kill* and *murder* occur in the Bible some 370 times. Life is a unique gift of God. He created us in His image. We are His and thus, only He has the authority to take life. Since we are His, He can say yes or no to our life.

God has delegated authority to legitimate government to take life: "Everyone must submit to the governing authorities, for there is no authority except from God, and those that exist are instituted by God. For government is God's servant for your good. But if you do wrong, be afraid, because it does not carry the sword for no reason. For government is God's servant, an avenger who brings wrath on the one who does wrong" (Romans 13:1, 4). We assume that government has the authority to have armies with personnel who kill the enemy in battle, to try people for murder, and to condemn them to death when they are found guilty. God instructed Moses and Joshua to kill the occupants of the land He had promised to Israel.

We are protected from the threat of death by an individual. The commandment makes no prohibition to the taking of life by governmental authority. There are references, in other Scripture, that provide for the taking of life under specific circumstances. For example, "Whoever sheds man's blood his blood will be shed by man, for God made man in His image" (Genesis 9:6, HCSB).

Jesus took this commandment and enlarged it. He describes the reasons or motivations behind the act of murder to deal with the feelings that cause killing, such as jealousy, hatred, and anger. Without this commandment it would be impossible for society to exist. Without it, only the strong would have any sense of security.

I was in the army in World War II. For a time in the Seventy-first Infantry Division I was a runner. My job was to take messages from one unit to another. We couldn't use radio for fear the Germans would intercept the messages. On one occasion I came across one of our half-track troop carriers that had been ambushed. There were eight or ten dead soldiers lying around on the ground. In that moment, and for a time, I was so angry that I could have killed anything German. If I had run across a noncombatant and killed him, I would have been guilty of murder. I would have done it out of anger.

Life is God's creation, and God has the right to make the rules. Disregard for life is the main reason for murders. Jesus said, "You have heard that it was said to our ancestors, **Do not murder,** and whoever murders will be subject to judgment. But I tell you, everyone who is angry with his brother will be subject to punishment" (Matthew 5:21–22, HCSB).

God expects His born-again children to work out their differences and be reconciled to each other. He expects us to be law-abiding citizens who depend on the government to decide who dies and who lives, rather than taking the law into our own hands.

Notes

Do Not Commit Adultery

The commandments against stealing, adultery, and coveting have much in common. The one guilty of adultery likely began by desiring a relationship with that man or woman and, when successful, stole the mate from the wife or husband. That man or woman is guilty of breaking three of the commandments: he or she is guilty of coveting, stealing, and adultery.

It is possible that the person has broken a fourth commandment as well. Making a graven image is giving authority to anything other than God. Lust has become an idol for people guilty of adultery.

Dishonoring one's father and mother may have occurred in the experience and thus would break a fifth commandment.

It is unlikely that the people involved could have gone through the experience without telling several lies. One very likely lie would be a fabrication about where they were on some occasions. This would be a sixth broken commandment.

It would not be very difficult to rule such a person guilty of breaking all Ten Commandments. Do not commit adultery. Protection of homes, families, children, and society are all involved in the commandment. We understand that divorce and disruption of the family was involved in the downfall of the Roman Empire.

In Old Testament times, adultery meant sexual relations outside of marriage involving a male Israelite, married or single, and the wife of another Israelite: "If a man commits adultery with a married woman—if he commits adultery with his neighbor's wife—both the adulterer and the adulteress must be put to death" (Leviticus 10:10, HCSB). Both were considered guilty since both were to be put to death.

Jesus expanded the commandment: "You have heard that it was said, do not commit adultery. But I tell you, everyone who looks at a woman to lust for her has already committed adultery with her in his heart" (Matthew 5:27–28, HCSB). We can admire someone without becoming lustful. It becomes lust when the person starts planning and taking steps to get involved privately with the person. The Muslims try to solve this problem by hiding women under hoods. I wonder if this doesn't create so much curiosity that men might take steps to get a look.

There is much in the Bible about marriage and husband-wife relationships that has multiple meanings. For instance, the church is the bride of Christ. In Ephesians 5 Paul equates husband-wife relationships to Christ's relationship with His bride the church.

This gives more importance to the need for stability of marriage. Adultery disrupts family life and makes it difficult for members to trust a heavenly Father and participate faithfully in church life.

> The seventh commandment is crucial.
> It safeguards the sanctity of marriage
> and protects the family and the home.

Notes

Do Not Steal

The commandment against stealing authorizes ownership. It forbids man or government to take away our right to have "stuff" and property. The legal way of acquiring property is by gifts from others and by honest work. The New Testament says this: "The thief must no longer steal. Instead he must do honest work with his own hands, so that he has something to share with anyone in need" (Ephesians 4:28, HCSB).

There are many ways to steal or take that which is not ours: outright stealing, picking pockets, pocketing stuff in stores, auto theft, and robbing banks or stores. One of my sons is ultra-honest. We were hiking one day, and he was ahead of me. I came across a coin and picked it up. I asked my son why he didn't pick it up. He said, "It wasn't mine."

There is the more hidden way of stealing, such as stealing from investors. Perhaps you've heard about Bernie Madoff, who swindled people out of sixty billion dollars, or of the Tennessee crook Dennis Bolze, who took only twenty million dollars. Don Cason, CEO of the Jefferson County Chamber of Commerce, said, "This has been a complete nightmare." He and his wife had invested with Bolze for several years. Madoff and Bolze are serving time.

There are employees who loaf on the job and employers who take advantage of their workers.

There is cheating on taxes. I heard of a man who counted money for his church. His hobby was coin collecting. He took all the change and reimbursed the church with a check. The trouble was that he claimed the check as a contribution and counted it as a deduction on his tax return.

There are employers who take advantage of their workers and employees who loaf on the job.

There is false advertising. There is borrowing books and not returning them. The New York City public library hired twelve detectives to recover books. Sometimes it is not stealing but just an oversight. My pastor returned from preaching a revival in another city. He brought back a book. Former members of our church had taken a church library book with them when they moved.

There is stealing from God: "Will a man rob God? Yet you are robbing Me!" You ask: "How do we rob you?" "By not making payments of 10 percent and the contributions" (Malachi 3:8, HCSB).

A professor in one of my classes at the University of Kentucky said, "No one is totally honest." This troubled me, so I asked Dr. Vernon Mussleman about it. He was another of my professors and one of our deacons at Immanuel Baptist Church. He said, "Keith, a person may not steal a thousand dollars, but he will take home a pencil from the office."

Stealing is an ancient vice. Jacob stole Esau's birthright with clever manipulation. We are told: "Differing weights are detestable to the Lord and dishonest scales are unfair" (Proverbs 20:23, HCSB). It must really grieve the Father when His children steal, whether it is the tithe or anything else.

Notes

Do Not Give False Testimony

"Do not give false testimony against your neighbor" (Exodus 20:16, HCSB). This could be the most crucial of the commandments. False witness is telling a lie where life or liberty could be at stake. Leaving false impressions can ruin someone's reputation. Telling a lie can be stealing a person's good name. Living a life that accurately represents our Savior is every Christian's responsibility.

When we claim one thing and live another, we can accurately be called a hypocrite. I have talked with people who are out of church and heard them blame the hypocrites. With nearly half the church members nongivers and absent from worship, there are plenty of hypocrites for the lost to use as an excuse for not believing.

A saved person is to be different from the world. A saved person is brand new. All things are new: "Therefore if any man is in Christ, he is a new creature; the old things passed away; behold new things have come" (2 Corinthians 5:17). He is now associated with Christ and His church. Whatever he does that casts a false impression on Jesus and His church is giving a false witness.

Of course the commandment includes the admonition to not tell lies. Leslie Flynn wrote a book titled *Did I Say That?*[24] One of the quotes from the book is about the man who had a "keen sense of rumor." We bear false witness when we repeat anything we have heard that is not 100 percent true. It is false witness when we deliberately leave a false impression to make ourselves look good or to make someone else look bad.

The opposite of bearing false witness is to bear a true witness. A true witness is one who loves his neighbor as himself, one who is faithful and supportive of the church, which is the body of Christ in this world. It is one who tells the truth in every circumstance and relationship. There are times when telling the truth would hurt someone. We should pray for God to give us good judgment about when to keep our mouths shut.

Then there are all the white lies. Someone asks you, "How are you?" and you say "fine" when you feel terrible. If we aren't careful, we end up splitting hairs and fearful of opening our mouths. "But no one can tame the tongue; it is a restless evil and full of deadly poison. With it we bless our Lord and Father and with it we curse men, who have been made in the likeness of God" (James 3:8–9).

We are obligated, as Christians, to keep the peace. It includes watching our tongues. Even our facial expressions or a wink can convey a wrong impression. We need to be straightforward and clear in all of our communications. May God help us to be honest in everything we say!

Notes

Do Not Covet

"Do not covet your neighbor's house. Do not covet your neighbor's wife, or his male or female slave, his ox or his donkey, or anything that belongs to your neighbor" (Exodus 20:17, HCSB). The purpose of the law is stated in Romans, where it is explained thusly: "What should we say then? Is the Law sin? Absolutely not! On the contrary, I would not have known sin if it were not for the law. For example, I would not have known what it is to covet if the law had not said, '**Do not covet**'" (Romans 7:7, HCSB).

According to the *Broadman Bible Commentary*[25] the word *covet* denoted not only an improper thought with regard to another's property, but included the overt attempt to take that property. There are some Scriptures that follow *covet* with *taking*: "You must burn up the carved images of their gods. Don't covet the silver or gold on the images or take it for yourself, or else you will be ensnared by it, for it is abhorrent to the Lord your God" (Deuteronomy 7:25, HCSB). Joshua said, "I coveted them and took them" (Joshua 7:21b, HCSB). If a person thinks the only way he can get what his neighbor has is by taking it from him, he is not trusting God to provide for him.

The previous commandments have forbidden acts. To disobey them is not likely to be a secret. One can covet, and at least initially, it can be a secret. Coveting begins in the mind and means "to set the heart on."

God is our source for everything. What we have comes from Him as He honors our honest labor. In Isaiah we find these words: "Seek the Lord … Instead of thornbush, a cypress will come up, and instead of the brier, a myrtle will come up" (Isaiah 55:6a, 13, HCSB). Thorns are mean things and myrtle is a beautiful wood. It is quite a contrast between depending on self to get things and depending on God. Myrtle wood grows only in southern Oregon, where I grew up, and in Palestine.

The result of coveting is a thorny experience that usually breaks other commandments such as lying, stealing, and adultery. This last commandment is closely linked to the first commandment, in which we are commanded to have no other gods but God. "But seek first the kingdom of God and His righteousness, and all these things will be provided for you" (Matthew 6:33, HCSB).

This commandment guards our hearts from greed. It reminds us to depend on God and our honest labor for the necessities of life. It can prevent us from stealing things that belong to others.

Without the cross, the **commandments** are a death sentence for all humanity but they make us know that we have fallen short of the glory of God. But thanks be to God for what we are promised: "Christ in you, the hope of glory" (Colossians 1:27b).

Notes

THE BEATITUDES

BEATITUDES

"Blessed are the poor in spirit for theirs is the kingdom of heaven" (Matthew 5:3). Poor in spirit means God is primary and everything else is secondary. Man's struggle in life is the tension between the physical and the spiritual. The physical aspects of life are kept in their place where they don't dominate us.

"Blessed are those who mourn, for they shall be comforted" (Matthew 5:4). These people are sorry for their sins. Being under conviction for sin is the first step toward a person's salvation.

"Blessed are the gentle, for they shall inherit the earth" (Matthew 5:5). This does not mean weakness! This person may be strong, but his strength is under God's control.

"Blessed are those who hunger and thirst for righteousness, for they shall be satisfied" (Matthew 5:6). Everyone enjoys being satisfied. It is not possible to be fully satisfied with unforgiven sin in our life.

"Blessed are the merciful for they shall receive mercy" (Matthew 5:7). These are people who are generous and compassionate toward others. They will receive mercy. It could mean "You reap what you sow." Jerry Sutton, one of my former pastors, on several occasions reminded us that not only do you reap what you sow, but you reap later than you sow, and you reap more than you sow.

"Blessed are the pure in heart, for they shall see God" (Matthew 5:8). This refers to the people who don't have ulterior motives; these people are good to others for the right reasons.

"Blessed are the peacemakers for they shall be called sons of God" (Matthew 5:9). These people work to create goodwill rather than strife in relationships. They seek to win people to Christ because the saved are the only people who know real peace.

"Blessed are those who have been persecuted for the sake of righteousness, for theirs is the kingdom of heaven" (Matthew 5:10). These are Christians who remain faithful to Christ in spite of danger or difficulty. These people would choose death before they would betray their Lord.

The beatitudes may be the path we follow from unsaved sinner to salvation. They can also be a formula for living that is productive and happy. Everyone wants to be happy. People try many ways to find happiness. Some of these are power, popularity, and pleasure.

God's way, which is outlined in the beatitudes, is the only certain, lasting way to be happy. God made us, and He knows what it takes for His created creatures to find happiness.

Notes

POOR IN SPIRIT

"And when He saw the multitudes, He went up on the mountain; and after He sat down, His disciples came to Him. And opening His mouth he began to teach them" (Matthew 5:1–2). This is a lesson, not a sermon.

"Blessed are the poor in spirit for theirs is the kingdom of heaven" (Matthew 5:3). This is the first of the beatitudes and a most important starting point. A proud person is not inclined to listen to good advice. These people are those who recognize their poor spiritual condition.

Blessed (happy) is the person who recognizes his own absolute helplessness, the one who puts his complete trust in God. This person will realize that material things will not produce happiness. He gives his allegiance to God, for he understands that God is the only source of genuine help and strength.

To him, things are unimportant and God is primary. This does not mean that material things don't have a place in life. Compassionate Christians help people who lack food, clothing, and shelter.

The poverty that is blessed is poverty of spirit that realizes man's inability to handle life without God's help. The Bible is not silent with respect to material things. Jesus said, "Do not be anxious, then, saying, 'What shall we eat?' or 'What shall we drink?' or 'With what shall we clothe ourselves?' For all these things the Gentiles eagerly seek; for your heavenly Father knows that you need all these things. But seek first His kingdom and His righteousness; and all these things shall be added to you" (Matthew 6:31 – 33).   In the Lord's Prayer we ask, "Thy kingdom come, Thy will be done on earth as it is in heaven." The kingdom of God is in the hearts of people where God's will is done on earth as it is in heaven. We can do God's will only when we realize our own inability to cope with life, and then put our whole trust in God.

The beatitudes outline the steps to salvation and the main aspects of a happy Christian life. This first beatitude recognizes that man is totally unable to deal with his sin, of which every person is guilty. It is only when we realize our hopeless condition, in that our sin separates us from God and thus will condemn us to an eternity in Hell unless it is dealt with, that we are willing to turn to God through faith in Jesus Christ, confessing our sin and asking for forgiveness.

On one occasion, when I was witnessing to my brother, he blurted out, "But I would have to give up too much." It is hard for a lost sinner to understand real happiness, the kind of happiness that comes when a person is born again through faith in Christ. The first step in that experience is conviction for sin. The Holy Spirit brings us to that conviction, and we swallow our pride and become poor in spirit.

Notes

Blessed Are They That Mourn

"Blessed are they that mourn, for they shall be comforted" (Matthew 5:4). Those who have lost a loved one understand what it is to mourn. It is a painful emotion evoked by losing a loved one. Mourning can refer to the emotion one experiences over the worst sorrow in life, but sorrow can be helpful. For one thing, it can make us appreciate some good things we tend to take for granted. An Arab proverb says, "All sunshine makes a desert."

Rain produces our food and flowers. Who would want perpetual sunshine? There are some understandings and experiences that only sorrow can produce. Loss can show us the love of our fellow men as they minister to us. My son lost his wife to a brain tumor. During the time she was ill, friends showered the family with food, prayers, and help with the seven children.

Sorrowful experiences can give us insights and understanding that we cannot get any other way. "Blessed be the God and father of our Lord Jesus Christ, the Father of mercies and God of all comfort; who comforts us in all of our afflictions so that we may be able to comfort those who are in any affliction with the comfort with which we ourselves are comforted by God" (2 Corinthians 1:3–4).   Sorrowful experiences can equip us to be ministers to others. Once we know how loss hurts, we are more likely to understand and have genuine sorrow for others who are going through the same type of experience. When we do minister to others and tell them we know how they feel, they will know that our comments are not just words.

God does not waste the experiences of His children. "And we know that God causes all things to work together for good to those who love God, to those who are called according to His purpose" (Romans 8:28). The next verse tells us what God sees as good. It is whatever makes us more like Jesus. Difficult experiences can help us be more patient and more understanding of others.

All of the above is true and has value, but the main meaning is "Blessed is the person who is desperately sorry for his own sin and unworthiness." The first step in salvation is repenting of our sin. The first beatitude dealt with our pride. With pride out of the way and recognizing our sinfulness and how it stands between us and God, we are ready to repent. Christianity begins with a sense of sin. Blessed

---

is the man who is intensely sorry for his sin. He has recognized the consequences of his sin that sent Jesus to a cruel death on the cross.

Blessed or happy is the person who mourns over his sin to such a degree that it compels him to confess his sin and trust Jesus for salvation.

Notes

MEEKNESS OR WEAKNESS

"Blessed are the gentle, for they shall inherit the earth" (Matthew 5:5). The King James Version uses *meek* instead of *gentle*. This is perhaps the most misunderstood of all the beatitudes. Many people think that to be meek is to be weak, and how could anyone want to be weak? We wish for ourselves and our children strength and self-reliance.

Another misconception about this beatitude is that it is a matter of disposition. We say, "She is easygoing, so it is simple for her to be meek." But is this true? Is it not that this meekness comes as a gift from God as a result of the new birth, and not because of one's disposition? We need to look at the meaning of the word translated "meek" in the New Testament. Ralph Sockman,[26] in *The Higher Happiness,* says that "The Hebrew word for meek is molded." When an individual submits himself completely to God, he allows God to mold his life, his actions, and his character.

Meekness means submission, but it is submission to God only. It does not mean a trod-upon, cowardly person who gives in to the cruel demands of others. Rather, one who is meek can with confidence say, like the apostle Paul, "I can do all things through Him who strengthens me" (Philippians 4:13). Neither does meekness mean that there has to be a passive resistance by the Christian. He must not seem weak or indifferent, since his strength comes from God; those who know him will respect him. It is a strength that, although long-suffering, can still stand up with the courage of its convictions. It is the strength of quiet fortitude that can endure difficulties, problems, and opposition because God is our refuge and strength.

Those who would serve God, and be an effective witness, must yield to God's molding. Before they can understand the needs of others, they must first accept the leadership of God in their lives. Those who want to make their service a spiritual ministry must submit themselves to God. We who have received Christ as Lord of our life no longer follow our own will but seek to know and do God's will. It is His loving guidance that molds the meek to inherit the earth. Is it possible to have the meekness Jesus spoke of in this beatitude? Is it possible for us to be meek like Jesus? The answer is yes. But it requires a willingness to be humble, give up self, and yield to God's will. When we are poor in spirit and have overcome our pride, when we mourn over our sins and have been comforted, and when God has tamed us, then we begin to live a meek life that overcomes the world. We are no longer subject to the temptations and troubles of a materialistic, sinful society. We are free to enjoy the beautiful Earth that God made for us.

Notes

Hungering After Righteousness

"Blessed are those who hunger and thirst for righteousness, for they shall be satisfied" (Matthew 5:6). Words have a context; they have meaning in keeping with the reputation of the speaker and the vocabulary of the ones who hear.

To those hearing Jesus, *hunger* and *thirst* didn't mean the same thing they mean to us. Many people in Palestine were never far from hunger or starvation. At that time, there was no plumbing where people could get a drink of water. In Jesus' day, many people were hungry much of the time. Being offered the possibility of eliminating hunger and thirst would really get their attention.

These people would know how much of a struggle it was to get food and water. Jesus was telling them that they should desire righteousness as much as they wanted food and water. Food and water really satisfy us when we are hungry and thirsty. Multitudes of people experience dissatisfaction in life. They seek satisfaction in material things and worldly pleasures. Even some Christians seek satisfaction in more stuff, popularity, and power. Jesus is saying that there is only one way to be really satisfied.

Without the righteousness of which Jesus speaks, there is no hope for satisfaction. Jesus speaks of the matter in another place: "Do not be anxious then, saying 'What shall we eat?' or 'What shall we drink?' or 'With what shall we clothe ourselves?' For all these things the Gentiles eagerly seek; for your heavenly Father knows that you need all these things. But seek first His kingdom and His righteousness; and all these things shall be added to you" (Matthew 6:31–33).

This beatitude tells us how strongly we should desire righteousness. Do we desire it as strongly as a starving person longs for food, and like one dying of thirst wants water? This beatitude expects much on our part, but it promises much.

It sets a goal, and makes a promise, but doesn't require us to reach the goal. It speaks of hungering and thirsting for it but doesn't require us to attain it. The only hope we have for righteousness is the gift of Christ's righteousness at the moment of our conversion. Once we are saved, this beatitude should take over. We are to grow in faith.

"So then, my beloved, just as you have always obeyed, not as in my presence only, but now much more in my absence, work out your salvation with fear and trembling; for it is God who is at work in you, both to will and to work for His good pleasure" (Philippians 2:12–13).

The Bible recognizes that we will not attain complete righteousness, but we still should desire it with all our heart. When we sin, God will cleanse us of it. "If we confess our sins, He is faithful and righteous to forgive us our sins and to cleanse us from all unrighteousness" (1 John 1:9).

Notes

Blessed Are the Merciful

"Blessed are the merciful, for they shall receive mercy" (Matthew 5:7). My first thought about this promise is that you reap what you sow. As stated in a previous devotional, my former pastors, Jerry Sutton, in several of his sermons reminded us that you not only reap what you sow, but reap later than you sow and more than you sow.

If we desire to be treated with mercy, we must be merciful. Even the greatest commandment alludes to it; we are to love our neighbor as ourselves. Jesus said, "For if you forgive men for their transgressions, your Heavenly Father will also forgive you. But if you do not forgive men, then your Father will not forgive your transgressions" (Matthew 5:14–15).

In the story of the unforgiving debtor, Jesus essentially says, you reap what you sow. He said, "So shall my heavenly Father also do to you, if each of you does not forgive his brother from your heart" (Matthew 18:35). The same principle is included in the Lord's Prayer: "And forgive us our debts as we also have forgiven our debtors" (Matthew 6:12). It would seem that the repetition of this thought in several different ways means that it is extremely important.

It is true in many cases that if we could know the reason why a person did what he did, we would probably be more sympathetic toward him. We can know that from personal experience. Who among us does not want to be understood? In our mind we may have said, "If the boss only knew what I'm going through at home."

We need to be better listeners. We need to do better at reading between the lines. We need to give the other person the benefit of the doubt. Many times, if we had only known what the other person had been through, we would have reacted differently.

The other side of the coin is that if the other person knew what I had just been through, he would understand my impatience or curt reply. The Bible touches on this in several places.

"Be angry, and yet do not sin; do not let the sun go down on your anger" (Ephesians 4:26). "But let everyone be quick to hear, and slow to anger; for the anger of man does not achieve the righteousness of God" (James 1:19b–20). The greatest commandment compels us to love others, even our enemies. This has to include being merciful.

God showed mercy when He sent His only begotten Son to die on a cruel cross, to save us from our sins. The very least we can do is to be merciful to the people around us. This certainly includes all fellow Christians. Jesus said to turn the other cheek. Not lashing out in retaliation, forgiving the other person, giving the benefit of the doubt, giving a helping hand, not getting even: all these could be showing mercy.

One last thought: the paramount consideration in every situation is our testimony. Will our words or actions help a lost person come to Christ? Will our words or our actions motivate another Christian to be more like Christ?

Notes

PURE IN HEART

"Blessed are the pure in heart, for they shall see God" (Matthew 5:8). To be pure is to be unadulterated. It is to be uncontaminated with foreign matter. How may our heart not be pure? Mixed motives, ulterior motives, and hidden motives are some of the possibilities. Blessed is the person whose reasons for what he does are always open and aboveboard. By *motive* we mean something that causes a person to act in a certain way or say what he says.

What are some of the reasons we do and say the things we do? The reasons can be positive or negative. Examples are hate, envy, spite, pride, getting even, bragging, fear, concern, humor, encouragement, compliment, or praise.

Andy Blaine, at a Baptist Student Union convention in Kentucky many years ago, said, "We never do anything for a completely unselfish reason. We helped someone out of concern, as a Christian should, but afterward we felt good for having done it. Or, we knew we'd feel guilty if we didn't do it."

Why do we do what we do? How do we feel after we have given to some worthy cause? Do we feel contented because we were generous or guilty because we didn't give enough? Do we go out of our way to help someone in need because we enjoy the praise for doing it, or because we will feel guilty if we don't do it?

We should ask ourselves these questions: Is our service given out of genuine concern, or because we'll enjoy the praise or pay to follow? Do we work in our church because Christ has called us to do it, or for the prestige we'll receive? Men have been known to serve as deacons because it gives them credibility. Why else do they accept the position and the title but fail to attend the meetings or do the work?

It is no easy thing to examine our motives. How can we not feel proud after we have done some good deed? In a church training group the members got into a discussion over whether a particular thing ought to be done out of a sense of duty even though a person didn't feel like doing it. The group was split on the answer.

What does the Bible say about our hearts? "The heart is more deceitful than all else and is desperately sick" (Jeremiah 17:9). David prayed, "Create in me a clean heart, O God, and renew a steadfast spirit within me" (Psalm 51:10).

God begins to work on our heart in the new birth experience, when we are first saved. He continues the work through the rest of our earthly life as the Holy Spit prompts us through prayer, Bible study, and worship experiences.

As for seeing God—whatever else it means, we know that after this life, everyone who has been born again by trusting Christ for salvation will see Him. A pure heart is one that has been changed by God through faith in Jesus Christ and cultivated thereafter through the presence and work of the Holy Spirit.

Notes

THE PEACEMAKERS

"Blessed are the peacemakers, for they shall be called the sons of God" (Matthew 5:9). Peace is a hoped-for condition that all people want. Peace doesn't always exclude problems or ensure the presence of tranquility. This beatitude pertains to the peacemaker. It doesn't include people with signs, demonstrating for peace in the street.

There are at least two types of peace: personal peace and public peace. The Bible is talking about personal peace, not peace among nations.

Peace is not a goal but the result of doing the right thing and being the right person. This beatitude is talking about the people whose life and actions produce peace. The peace that the Bible calls blessed does not come from avoiding problems. It comes from having a right relationship with God and doing His will. Blessed are the peacemakers, for they do God's work in the world.

When the angel announced the Lord's birth, he said, "Glory to God in the highest, and on earth peace among men with whom He is well pleased" (Luke 2:14). Jesus said, "Peace I leave with you; My peace I give to you; not as the world gives, do I give to you. Let not your heart be troubled, nor let it be afraid" (John 14:27). God did not promise peace for everyone. He announced peace for those with whom He is well pleased.

The kind of peace that the angels announced is the kind of peace that Jesus possessed. Jesus said, "*My peace* I give to you." Jesus had peace because He always did the will of His Father. We have this peace as a gift from Jesus when we abide by His will and do His work.

Paul speaks of peace in several places: "Now the God of peace be with you all" (Romans 15:33). "Now may the God of peace Himself sanctify you entirely; and may your spirit and soul and body be preserved complete, without blame at the coming of our Lord Jesus Christ" (1 Thessalonians 5:23).

Peace comes from a right relationship with God who is the God of peace and thus the source of peace.

Many churches experience conflict. Sometimes this is because members have the freedom to speak their minds and often have different opinions about a matter. Some people have a knack for saying the right thing at the right time, to help the congregation settle down and arrive at a peaceful solution. Such a person is a peacemaker.

The beginning of peace for any person is salvation through faith in Jesus Christ. We are peacemakers when we witness to unsaved people and help them come to Christ.

Notes

THE PERSECUTED

"Blessed are those who have been persecuted for the sake of righteousness, for theirs is the kingdom of heaven" (Matthew 5:10). Jesus knew those who followed Him would be persecuted, for he said, "Blessed are you when men revile you, and persecute you, and say all kinds of evil against you falsely on account of Me" (Matthew 5:11). He followed this statement with a promise of reward for those who were persecuted: "Rejoice and be glad, for your reward in heaven is great, for so they persecuted the prophets who were before you (Matthew 5:12).

The first Christians experienced immense suffering. Nero is supposed to have lined the highway with Christians on crosses. How could they do their work or enjoy any kind of home life when men like Saul of Tarsus went about putting them in prison? Jesus knew that even members of a person's family would betray them. "And brother will deliver up brother to death, and a father his child; and children will rise up against parents, and cause them to be put to death" (Matthew 10:21). Jesus said that these people could still be blessed or happy.

The world today has many examples of Christians being persecuted. Thousands of people, like those in the Sudan, have been killed. Even though South Sudan has become an independent nation, the Muslims in the north are still killing them, especially in border areas where there are oil wells. Muslims who become Christians are in danger of being killed.

The story of Polycarp, the aged priest of Smyrna, is the story of one of the more famous martyrs. He was given the choice of sacrificing to the godhead of Caesar or die. His reply: "Eighty and six years have I served Christ and He has done me no wrong. How can I blaspheme my King who saved me?" So they brought him to the stake and he prayed his last prayer. "O Lord God Almighty, the Father of thy well-beloved and ever-blessed Son, by whom we have received the knowledge of Thee ... I thank Thee that Thou hast thought me worthy of this day and this hour."

The Christian who suffers for his faith can say, "Brothers, we are treading where the saints have trod." Early in our history some Christians suffered persecution because they didn't belong to the right denomination. Some of them stood their ground and made it easier for us who followed.

We enjoy our freedom because those in the past were willing to take a stand at a personal cost to themselves. How are Christians in America persecuted today? It is not like anything in the past. We are not likely to be killed. For most of us, the worst thing we experience may be some ridicule. Some Christians could be punished by their bosses in some way if they refuse to work on Sunday.

Jesus needs those who are not so much prepared to die for Him as to live for Him. Our home is not this world. We know we have a wonderful future with the Lord. This life can be tough, but it is brief compared with eternity. We are part of the kingdom of God.

Notes

FRUIT OF THE SPIRIT

SPIRITUAL FRUIT

"The fruit of the Spirit is love, joy, peace, patience, kindness, goodness, faith, gentleness, self-control. Against such things there is no law" (Galatians 5:22–23, HCSB). The book of Galatians was written by Paul to rescue people from error. They were being misled by the Judaizers, who were trying to convince new Christians that to please God they had to be circumcised and obey the Law. Paul called them foolish to have begun by the Spirit but to think that obedience to rules and ceremonies meant they were being perfected and made mature.

Paul was telling them that holiness is what God plants in the heart and that the result is like a seed that grows and produces fruit. "The man who trusts in the Lord, whose confidence indeed is the Lord, He will be like a tree planted by water: it sends its roots out toward a stream, it doesn't fear when heat comes, and its foliage remains green. It will not worry in a year of drought or cease producing fruit" (Jeremiah 17:1–8, HCSB). Possessing the characteristics, described by the "fruit of the spirit," means the Christian can weather all kinds of bad circumstances with a smile and a positive spirit.

"Either make the tree good and its fruit good, or make the tree bad, and its fruit bad; for the tree is known by its fruit" (Matthew 12:33, HCSB). We must realize that we influence people around us. We represent Jesus once we have received Him as our Savior. How people view us will determine whether we have a positive or a negative influence. Having a part in another person's decision to accept Christ as Savior is one type of fruit that we bear. Another way to think about it is "the fruit of a Christian is another Christian." Jesus explains the parable of the sower: "But the seed in the good ground—these are the ones who, having heard the word with an honest and good heart, and hold on to it and by enduring, bear fruit" (Luke 8:15, HCSB).

Ephesians tells us, "For you were once darkness, but now you are light in the Lord. Walk as children of light—for the fruit of the light results in all goodness, righteousness and truth—discerning what is pleasing to the Lord" (Ephesians 5:8–10, HCSB).

The fruit of the Spirit is singular. It is a package of traits. This means, for example, that we cannot have patience if we don't have love, and we cannot have peace if we don't have self-control, and we cannot have joy if we don't have goodness. Developing and maturing these traits that God plants in our heart at salvation is what occurs in sanctification or Christian growth. "For it is God who is working in you, (enabling you) both to will and to act for His good purpose" (Philippians 2:13, HCSB). What God needs is our cooperation. We cooperate when we pray, study His word, listen to sermons, and respond to the impressions He gives us in the process.

Notes

LOVE

The Bible tells us that "Love is patient, love is kind, and is not jealous; love does not brag and is not arrogant, does not act unbecomingly; it does not seek its own, is not provoked, does not take into account a wrong suffered, does not rejoice in unrighteousness, but rejoices in the truth; bears all things, believes all things, hopes all things, endures all things" (1 Corinthians 13:4–7). Verse 8 begins with "Love never fails" but says that gifts like prophecy and tongues will cease.

Agape is a word for love that is totally different from the way the world defines love. It is God-like. It is God's love for us and the kind of love that God expects from us. Agape is the love that is included in the fruit of the Spirit. Agape love defines the greatest commandment. Understanding agape helps us know how we are to treat everyone, including our enemies.

Romantic love, eros, is conditioned by agape. Sexual abuse and infidelity are definitely not in the best interests of the other person. When we fail to do that which is in the best interest of the other person, we have not been what love in the fruit of the Spirit requires of us.

The desire for personal satisfaction is such a strong emotion that it can dominate a life. It can be so strong that a person will use any means to please himself.

When we have been wronged, there is a strong desire to get even. Agape love forbids any effort to get even. Jesus demonstrated such love when He asked the Father to forgive those who nailed Him to the cross. Nothing we ever face in life will be as difficult as that.

As with other emotions, we may not feel like doing the right thing, but we can perform the required action and the emotion will follow. I once took the Dale Carnegie course. One of the projects was to make a one-minute speech, beating the table with a rolled-up newspaper and pretending we were mad. I don't get angry easily, but I decided to speak about an accident that had injured a little girl. By pretending I was mad and beating the table with the newspaper, I was genuinely mad less than thirty seconds into my speech.

It would not be hypocritical to exercise agape love toward a neighbor even if he was an "ornery old cuss." Just act like you "love" your neighbor. If you do this, you will discover a great truth, when you act like you love someone, you will soon come to love that person.

If we get even with someone who has harmed us, it will not help us love him as we are commanded to do. If we do something helpful for him, we may find we begin to like him. We need to be reminded over and over that agape love does that which is in the best interest of the other person. It may be hard to know what is in the best interests of the other person, but we are obligated to try. Through prayer and God's help, we will be able to do it.

Notes

Joy

"These things I have spoken to you, that My joy may be in you, and that your joy may be made full" (John 15:11). Only those who have experienced the grace of God in salvation can know the kind of joy that is spoken of by John. It is a natural condition resulting from love in the heart. Since it comes from God's grace, we can weather serious storms in life without drowning in grief and sadness. It is a sense of peace and satisfaction that is unrelated to circumstances.

When we study the Scriptures and realize the good news of the gospel, we can't help but experience a joy that does pass understanding. Added to that is the environment that we live in by associating with fellow Christians in Bible study, worship, and other church activities. "What we have seen and heard we proclaim to you also that you may have fellowship with us so that our joy made be made complete" (1 John 1:4).

We remember the joy of salvation when we realize that our sins have been forgiven and God remembers them no more. Those who hurt the most, because of their sin, sense the most joy about being forgiven. I love this verse in "There Is a Fountain." "The dying thief rejoiced to see That fountain in his day; And there may I, though vile as he, Wash all my sins away."[27]

The joy of the early believers resulted from a great sense of relief at Christ's resurrection. They also saw Him ascend into heaven and remembered His promise to return. The fact that so many saw him, and that their testimony is reported in Scripture, should give us confidence that our faith is not in vain.

Our joy has the same source, as it is passed on to us through the Bible. And much more, because the Scriptures tell us that all that is—this world and all that is in it—was made by Him. To know that we are God's handiwork and not the result of mindless matter sloshing around until it made life gives us a great sense of worth.

Just to observe God's provision in creation should thrill our hearts: think of all that exists in minerals and metals, food and flowers, sunshine and rain, fish and fowl, and much more. God made us with minds and eyes and ears and hands, and the ability to appreciate and manipulate all that He made to produce the stuff of modern life.

That all this came to be without a designer, a creator, is infinitely impossible.

To think that we are the children of this great Creator enables us to face all adversity with joy—heavenly joy.

Notes

Peace

Jesus said, "Peace I leave with you; My peace I give to you; not as the world gives, do I give to you. Let not your heart be troubled, nor let it be fearful" (John 14:27). The world describes peace as the absence of tension or the cessation of hostilities. Jewish people greet each other with the word *shalom,* meaning "peace."

A dictionary definition of *peace* is "freedom from anxiety, annoyance or other mental disturbance." The Lord says, "Thus sayeth the Lord thy Redeemer, the Holy one of Israel; I am the Lord thy God which teacheth thee to profit, which leadeth thee by the way that thou shouldest go. O that thou hadst hearkened to my commandments! Then had thy peace been as a river, and thy righteousness as the waves of the sea" (Isaiah 48–49, KJV).

There can be no peace, or sense of well-being, when it seems like everything is chaotic and out of control. Following God's guidance is the only long-lasting way to keep everything under control. This is obtained by looking to the Lord, through prayer and Bible study, and giving Him our allegiance so He can teach us what is good and help us know the way we should go.

The society in which we live makes it difficult. Our society operates in a way that is contrary to scriptural standards. Through advertising on television, and in magazines and newspapers, we are peppered with colorful ads that tell us that peace and happiness come through a good salary, health insurance, a home that is at least as nice as our neighbor's, fashionable clothing, good food, and a new automobile.

All of the above involves dependence on money, our ability, and other people. Jesus had nowhere to lay His head, and yet He epitomized peace. He told us to live in the world but not of the world. We should not look to other people or the government to provide personal peace.

Biblical peace is secured by following God's instruction for living. He created us and knows what is best for us. We know that our future is secure because we have placed our faith in the Lord Jesus, who is the Prince of Peace.

God's way is spelled out in the Bible. "Be anxious for nothing, but in everything by prayer and supplication with thanksgiving let your requests be made known to God. And the peace of God, which surpasses all comprehension, shall guard your hearts and your minds in Christ Jesus" (Philippians 4:6–7).

Notes

PATIENCE

Patience improves with practice. For some it may mean counting to ten before responding. Doing so gives a person time to think about the consequences of a rash response. This means that we handle slowly our response to the things that aggravate or irritate us.

The reason for our emotion may be a real wrong, but our reaction to it, if slow enough, gives us time to avoid making matters worse. God is our model: "The Lord, the Lord God, compassionate and gracious, slow to anger, and abounding in loving-kindness and truth" (Exodus 34:6).

Some people may think anger is a sin, but James indicates otherwise: "But let everyone be quick to hear, slow to speak and slow to be angry, for the anger of man does not achieve the righteousness of God" (James 1:9b–20). When we practice the presence of God, we are always reminded that our witness is at stake, and this should temper our response. The Bible says, "Be angry, and yet do not sin; do not let the sun go down on your anger, and do not give the devil an opportunity" (Ephesians 4:26–27). We need to remember that the devil is still going about trying to do us damage.

King Saul could not wait for Samuel to arrive, and in his impatience he offered burnt offerings. As a result, his sons would not follow him to the throne.

Then there was Peter, who cut off the ear of the soldier who was arresting Jesus. Some may have considered Peter a hero, but Jesus rebuked him. Jesus came to save us. To act rashly and impatiently might mean the loss of an opportunity to witness for Christ. Maintaining our testimony is vital.

Impatience with each other in the life of the church is divisive and disruptive. True patience cannot be attained by human effort. It is a fruit cultivated in the believer by the indwelling Holy Spirit. Patience doesn't stand alone. Without kindness, love, knowledge, faith, and hope, one cannot be patient.

We can be patient, if we take time to understand what is going on in a given situation. Ignorance, not knowing all the facts in a given event, prompts impatience.

"Tribulation worketh patience" (Roman 5:3, KJV). Children are impatient, in part, because they lack experience and knowledge. Some adult Christians haven't matured in the faith. Mature Christians should be patient with them. We witness to each other when we are patient with each other. Experience and knowledge and tested faith in the Lord enable us to be more patient.

Patience is almost synonymous with waiting. Scripture advises us to wait on the Lord: "Wait for the Lord; Be strong, and let your heart take courage; Yes, wait for the Lord" (Psalm 27:14).

Notes

KINDNESS

The King James Version doesn't use the word *kindness* but speaks of gentleness and goodness. Perhaps we don't need technical definitions for a word like *kindness*. We read in Galatians, "But the fruit of the Spirit is love, joy, peace, patience, kindness, goodness, faithfulness, gentleness, self-control; against such there is no law" (Galatians 5:22–23). Most of us have used the word or heard it used many times.

We see acts of kindness all around us, if we are alert. Jesus spoke of giving food to the hungry and visiting the sick. We should be alert to people who are in trouble and do what we can to help them. A selfish person tends to be unkind because he thinks too highly of himself. He occupies his time and uses his resources on his own needs and interests. With his attention on self he doesn't see, or he ignores, the problems of others.

Such a person may be kind, on occasion, because kindness can be a means of getting what he wants. Jacob showed kindness to Esau and then stole his birthright. Jael gave Sisera a bottle of milk and then drove a tent peg through his temple. We read about that in Judges chapter 4.

Kindness is a quality of God. The potential for kindness is in us as an element of being born again. "Therefore if any man is in Christ, he is a new creature; the old things passed away; behold new things have come" (2 Corinthians 5:17). Those new things include the fruit of the Spirit.

One of the most notable examples of kindness is that of the Good Samaritan. The priest and the Levite were too intent on their own business to stop and take time to help a man in need. Perhaps they were late for the prayer meeting at the synagogue. They might have been afraid of getting their hands dirty by helping a man in the ditch. Pride and selfishness go together and so do humility and kindness. The Samaritan, unlike the priest and Levite, put aside his own needs to minister to the man in the ditch.

One of the most needful places for being kind to one another is in the church, the Body of Christ. We are salt and light in the world, and acts of kindness may very well be like salt and light. You may have seen on TV a feature showing acts of kindness such as helping a person who is crippled across a busy street. I don't know who sponsors the show, but it is a good thing. Our acts of kindness can have eternal results, because sometimes such acts give us the opportunity to share the gospel of Christ. "And be kind to one another, tender-hearted, forgiving each other, just as God in Christ has forgiven you" (Ephesians 4:32).

Notes

FAITH

Faith flows from faith in God. When our attention is focused on Him, steadfastness and dependability develops as His claims and His law determine our actions and demeanor. When faith is absent, disobedience, deceit, and dishonesty are present. The person of faith has direction in life that provides predictability and accountability. This is in contrast to the life that is tossed about by shifting winds of circumstance and emotional impulses.

Every aspect of the Christian life depends on faith. Some of these are financial stewardship, prayer, church attendance, punctuality, witnessing, encouraging others, serving, and preparation for Bible study.

Think of the things and situations we depend on to be faithful and trustworthy: the spinning of Earth, sunrise and sunset, the air we breathe, the water we drink, the food we eat, banks, people, our spouses, friends, planes, traffic, police, and above all our heavenly Father. God is faithful. "Let us hold fast the confession of our hope without wavering, for He who promised is faithful" (Hebrews 10:23).

"His work is perfect, for all His ways are just; A God of faithfulness and without injustice, Righteous and upright is He" (Deuteronomy 32:4). "Thy loving-kindness, O Lord, extends to the heavens, Thy faithfulness reaches to the skies" (Psalm 36:5). "His faithfulness is a shield and bulwark" (Psalm 91:4b). "The Lord is good; His loving-kindness is everlasting and His faithfulness to all generations" (Psalm 100:5).

We have a God who is described in these verses as perfect, just, good, faithful, a bulwark, and everlasting. It seems there are insufficient superlatives to describe our Savior and our God. God is our model. "For whom He foreknew, He also predestined to become conformed to the image of His son, that He might be the first- born among many brethren" (Romans 8:29). Our faith grows stronger as God helps us to become more like Jesus. Scripture tells us to walk by faith, live by faith, stand by faith, pray in faith, and overcome through faith. Words that are related to faith are *steady, loyal, reliable, trustworthy, constant, stable,* and *dependable.*

There is a poem that describes the faithful few. They are the ones who can be counted on to do the work of a church: to visit, minister, teach, usher, and sing in the choir, be faithful in attendance, and be generous givers. They don't make excuses or let the things of the world distract them.

Our faith in God may be no bigger than a mustard seed in the beginning, but it must grow if we are to live a life that honors God and bears fruit. And it will grow as we experience God's faithfulness and respond to it.

Notes

Gentleness or Meekness

Gentleness, meekness, and humility are closely related. These are far from weakness because to be properly performed, gentleness requires great strength. God has a purpose for every believer, and He promises us power like that which raised Jesus from the dead. We read, "the surpassing greatness of His power toward us who believe ... brought about by the strength of His might when He raised Him from the dead ... and He put all things under His feet, and gave Him as head over all things to the church, which is His body" (Ephesians 1:19–23).

God's purpose for us is related to Christ's body, the church. His power enables us to be effective in all we do to build up the church. What a shame it is when proud people get into angry arguments in church business meetings.

Moses was commended for his meekness, yet he led a nation out of slavery in Egypt. God said of him, "Now the man Moses was very humble, more than any man on the face of the earth" (Numbers 12:3, HCSB). Man's humility and God's strength is an unbeatable combination.

Jesus, according to all that we know about Him, demonstrated this trait and describes this attribute: "Come to me, all of you who are weary and burdened, and I will give you rest. All of you, take up my yoke and learn from Me, because I am gentle and humble of heart, and you will find rest for yourselves" (Matthew 11:28–29, HCSB). The kind of rest that we have in Christ enables us to avoid ulcer-causing agitation and fingernail-biting stress.

Scripture tell us, "Always being ready to make a defense to everyone who asks you to give an account for the hope that is in you, yet with gentleness and reverence" (1 Peter 3:15). We need knowledge of Scripture that enables us to explain why we are Christians, but our explanations must be calm with a quiet confidence.

In Peter 2:21–24 we are told that Christ is our example who committed no sin and that while being reviled, He uttered no threats and bore our sins on the cross that we might die to sin and live to righteousness.

We will never face a situation as severe as Jesus endured on the cross. What an example for us as He prayed for those who nailed Him to the cross. With Jesus as our example, we should be able to avoid angry responses to slights and insults.

Psalm 37:11 reminds us that "the humble will inherit the land and will delight themselves in abundant prosperity." To be a meek, gentle, and humble person requires complete submission to God. It doesn't mean submission to people who try to dominate us. With God's help, we are to control our response to such people so that anger or rage do not take over and cause us to destroy our witness and make matters worse.

Notes

SELF-CONTROL

You would think that if a person practiced love, joy, peace, patience, kindness, goodness, faithfulness, and gentleness, he or she should have no problem with self-control. We need to be reminded that it is the fruit of the Spirit, not fruits. They come together as a package. Self-control is managing life and freedom in an orderly manner. God gave us the freedom of choice or self-will. God could have made us robots, like lower animals, living by instinct so that our love of God would have been automatic. If He had done that, our love and obedience would have been meaningless.

We live life with two choices. One is the *narrow* way and the other the *broad* way. There are two choices on the narrow way. One is legalistic with strict rules that govern every aspect of life. The second is Jesus' way, where we are led by the Holy Spirit and the Scriptures. The broad way is the way of the world where people do whatever their emotions allow. Both the broad way and the legalistic way lead to destruction.

The book of Romans gives us some guidance: "The faith that you have, have as your own conviction before God. Happy is he who does not condemn himself in what he approves. But he who doubts is condemned if he eats, because his eating is not of faith; and whatever is not from faith is sin" (Romans 14:22–23).

One of the restraints on us is the way we think about the things we do. Romans 14:14 reads, "I know and am convinced in the Lord Jesus that nothing is unclean in itself; but to him who thinks anything is unclean, to him it is unclean."

Another restraint has to do with the effect our actions have on a weaker Christian: "It is good not to eat meat or to drink wine, or to do anything by which your brother stumbles" (Romans 14:21).

Peter repeats some of the fruit of the Spirit: "Now for this very reason also, applying all diligence, in your faith supply moral excellence, and in your moral excellence, knowledge; and in your knowledge, self-control, and in your self-control, perseverance and in your perseverance, godliness; and in your godliness, brotherly kindness and in your brotherly kindness, Christian love" (2 Peter 1:5–7).

Some of the attitudes and actions that self-control help us avoid are hatred, discord, jealousy, rage, selfish ambition, factions, envy, worry, fear, critical spirit, gossip, and greed. Without the new-birth experience, self-control would be impossible. Even so, we must be on our guard and work at this part of the fruit.

Some people are mild tempered, whereas others have a "short fuse." We are all different, but we are all under the same scriptural challenge. Christian growth includes, if it is not totally identified by, how well we "grow" the fruit of the Spirit.

Notes

Holidays

New Year's Resolutions

Perhaps a majority of people make New Year's resolutions. Very likely those resolutions include lose weight, get organized, exercise more and get out of or reduce debt. Here are some biblical possibilities for New Year's resolutions:

Pray more: "Be anxious for nothing, but in everything by prayer and supplication with thanksgiving let your requests be made know to God" (Philippians 4:6). Pray more and pray more intelligently. One preacher said we should seek more information about the concerns we have, so that we can know better how to pray. Some people keep a prayer diary to help them remember what to pray for and to be reminded of answered prayers.

Serve more: "Therefore, my beloved brethren, be steadfast, immovable, always abounding in the work of the Lord, knowing that your toil is not in vain in the Lord" (1 Corinthians 15:58). Always abounding! Are we really using our time in a way that is well pleasing to the Lord? For many of us there is much more we could be dong in the Lord's service.

Give more: "Now this I say, he who sows sparingly shall also reap sparingly; and he who sows bountifully shall also reap bountifully. Let each one do just as he has purposed in his heart; not grudgingly or under compulsion; for God loves a cheerful giver" (2 Corinthians 9:6–7). How about reading a book on biblical stewardship to help find out if you are anywhere near where you ought to be in your giving? Start with the tithe and grow from there. "'Bring the whole tithe into the storehouse, so that there may be food in My house, and test Me now in this,' says the Lord of hosts, 'if I will not open for you the windows of heaven, and pour out for you blessing until there is no more need'" (Malachi 3:10).

Study more: "Be diligent to present yourself approved to God as a workman who does not need to be ashamed, handling accurately the word of truth" (2 Timothy 2:15). Do we use Bible-study helps? Have we investigated how to study the Bible? Perhaps we should study more intelligently, not just study more.

Witness more: "I have become all things to all men, that I may by all means save some" (1 Corinthians 9:22b). Paul really worked at witnessing. He thought about the people he wanted to share Christ with and then adjusted his approach to them so he could get their attention and confidence, thus giving him a better chance to reach them.

Most of us need to not only witness more, but witness more intelligently.

Notes

SERVE MORE

"Therefore, my dear brothers, be steadfast, immovable, always excelling in the Lord's work, knowing that your labor in the Lord is not in vain" (1 Corinthians 15:58, HCSB). What is the work of the Lord? Jesus declared, "I will build my church, and the forces of Hades will not overpower it" (Matthew 16:18b, HCSB). "Based on the gift each one has received, use it to serve others, as good managers of the varied grace of God" (1 Peter 4:10, HCSB).

Our work is to help Christ build His church. One of the ways we can do that is to use the spiritual gift(s) God has given us to serve others. Every Christian receives at least one such gift. It seems that other people sometimes know what our spiritual gift is better than we do. Ask your friends what they think yours is.

"For we are His creation, created in Christ Jesus for good works, which God prepared ahead of time so that we should walk in them" (Ephesians 2:10, HCSB). Too many people stop with verse 9. We need more "Ephesians 2:10" Christians.

There is a list of spiritual gifts in the twelfth chapter of Romans. Some of the spiritual gifts are prophecy, service, faith, teaching, exhortation, giving, leading, and showing mercy. Surely everyone has at least one of these and can put it to work helping His church in reaching out to the lost and ministering to people in need.

There are many ways to help. We can be friendly with everyone and welcome newcomers and visitors to church. Leaders and church staff members always appreciate a word of encouragement or a deserved compliment.

Picking up trash helps keep the place clean and pleases the janitor. Every church member should pay attention to who is missing and take steps to encourage them to return. You might be a buddy to someone, perhaps to a new Christian.   "Whatever you do, do it enthusiastically, as something done for the Lord and not for men" (Colossians 3:23, HCSB). Our service should be enthusiastic and wholehearted.

When we keep in mind that what we do is for the Lord, it should help us feel better about what we do. When I took that Dale Carnegie course, I discovered something about emotions. Even if you are not an enthusiastic person by nature, you can push yourself to be so and the first thing you know your enthusiasm will be genuine.

Every Christian should take the Great Commission seriously. Jesus' admonition as He prepared to return to the Father was for His disciples to go, or as some interpret it to mean, "as you go." As we go about our daily work, or play, or mission trips, or vacation, we should always be prepared to share with others what Jesus has done for us. This is the most important thing we can do as we work under the leadership of Jesus to build His church.

Notes

Pray More

"Don't worry about anything, but in everything, through prayer and petition with thanksgiving; let your request be made known to God" (Philippians 4:6, HCSB). Praying about everything can mean that as we go about our work and play, we have our minds set on God. It goes like this: We see something beautiful in nature and praise God for it; we face a problem and ask God for help; we flare up in anger and ask to be forgiven. *The Practice of the Presence of God*, the title of Brother Lawrence's book, would be *the same concept as* praying about everything.

Another verse that implies living in an attitude of prayer is "Give thanks in everything, for this is God's will for you in Christ Jesus" (1 Thessalonians 5:18, HCSB). As bad as some situations can be, it is amazing how we can find something for which to be thankful if we really think about it. We are not to give thanks *for* everything but *in* everything.

Here is another prayer promise: "Keep asking and it will be given to you. Keep searching, and you will find. Keep knocking and the door will be opened to you" (Matthew 7:7, HCSB). This promise says we should persist in prayer. It is interesting to note that, at least in English, the verse makes an acrostic of the word *ask*. Prayer should be a habit. We are told to "Pray constantly" (1 Thessalonians 5:17, HCSB). Most of us have probably been encouraged many times to have a quiet time early in the morning. That is good, but we may need to pray many times during the day as we go about our work and play just as much. Waiting until morning might mean we forget some things, and by then it may be too late to pray for other needs.

Habits are difficult to develop and harder to maintain but are essential if we want to do something consistently. Someone said that to develop a new habit, we have to work at it for six weeks, working at it by tying a string around our finger or using some other reminder. Let's work on our prayer habit. We don't have to quit what we are doing, or kneel, or say it out loud in order to pray. We can just say it in our mind.

The Bible contains a strong emphasis on prayer: *pray, prayers,* and *praying* appear about 470 times. The model prayer gives us a good list of things to remember when we pray. One thought comes to mind as we look at the model prayer. It is brief. Perhaps we should pay more attention to the sincerity of our prayers rather than to the length of our prayers.

"Therefore, you should pray like this: Our Father in heaven, Your name be honored as holy. Your kingdom come. Your will be done on earth as it is in heaven. Give us today our daily bread. And forgive us our debts, as we have forgiven our debtors. And do not bring us into temptation, but deliver us from the evil one. For Yours is the kingdom and the power and the glory forever. Amen" (Matthew 6:9–13, HCSB).

Notes

GIVE MORE

Shortly after I was saved my brother went with me to church. As I dropped a sizable bill in the offering plate, my brother whispered in my ear, "Are you crazy?" My brother still isn't saved after all these years. For some unknown reason, I took the tithe for granted from the very beginning of my Christian life. The only Bible study I was exposed to, before age twenty-two, was at a couple of vacation Bible schools in the Applegate, Oregon, public school building. I was nine and ten years old. The teacher must have taught tithing.

"'Bring the whole tithe into the storehouse, so that there may be food in my house, and test Me now in this,' says the Lord of hosts, 'if I will not open you the windows of heaven, and pour out for you a blessing until there is no more need'" (Malachi 3:10). It seems to me that for us Christians, the local church is the storehouse. In my life there is ample evidence that God does bless the tither.

In Genesis 14:18–20, we learn that Melchizedek, a priest of God, received tithes from Abraham. In Hebrews 7:17 we are told that Jesus was a high priest after the order of Melchizedek. The only thing we know about Melchizedek is that he had no beginning and no ending and he received tithes from Abraham. When we give to our church, we are giving to Jesus, who is busy building His church.

Jesus endorsed the tithe: "Woe to you scribes and Pharisees, hypocrites! For you tithe mint and dill and cumin, and have neglected the weightier provisions of the law: justice and mercy and faithfulness; but these are things you should have done without neglecting the others" (Matthew 23:23).

Apparently liberal giving is a spiritual gift. Paul says, "Since we have gifts that differ according to grace given us, let each exercise them accordingly—he who gives, with liberality" (Romans 12:6, 8). Some people have a gift of making money and giving it away; may their tribe increase. But this doesn't let us who may not have a gift of making money off the "tithing hook." The tithe is where giving begins and offerings follow.

Farmers know that sowing sparingly results in a meager harvest. Scripture says, "Now this I say, he who sows sparingly shall also reap sparingly; and he who sows bountifully shall also reap bountifully. Let each one do just as he has purposed in his heart; not grudgingly or under compulsion; for God loves a cheerful giver" (2 Corinthians 9:6–7).

We are told in 2 Corinthians 8:2 that the Macedonians "overflowed in the wealth of their liberality." They gave beyond their ability. They gave sacrificially. Then in Philippians 4:19 we get the rest of the story. "And my God shall supply all your needs according to His riches in glory in Christ Jesus." Some people try to generalize the 4:19 verse, but I believe it applies to those who are sacrificial givers.

May God help us to *give more*!

Notes

STUDY MORE

Are we too old to grow to grow spiritually, to change, or to learn? They say you can't teach old dogs new tricks, but we are not dogs. What happens to our bodies if we sit and lie around all the time? Our minds need exercise just like our bodies. "Be diligent to present yourself approved to God as a workman who does not need to be ashamed, handling accurately the word of truth" (2 Timothy 2:15). The King James Version says *study* instead of *be diligent*. Do you know anyone who understands the entire Bible? The longer we live, the more we experience and observe, and this gives us more to think about in our Bible study.

Bible study is a lifelong task. "Work out your salvation with fear and trembling; for it is God who is at work in you, both to will and to work for His good pleasure" (Philippians 2:12b–13). After we are saved, God works in us to help us become all we can be. Our job is to cooperate with our heavenly Father.

"Without consultation, plans are frustrated, But with many counselors they succeed" (Proverbs 15:22). Do you have a dictionary to look up strange words? The larger our vocabulary, the more able we are to understand what we read and what we hear in sermons and lectures. Do you use your church library? The library can be a great source of *counselors*. The authors of books share with us from their study, research and experience. What do you do with your questions, curiosity, and problems? The Bible and Bible-study helps are tools to help us find answers to our questions and problems.

"For I am confident of this very thing, that He who began a good work in you will perfect it until the day of Jesus Christ" (Philippians 1:6). Remember! God is at work in us. He is working, and we need to help Him by doing what we can. We can develop our understanding of His Word and apply it to our lives as we come to understand His perfect will.

"I press on toward the goal for the prize of the upward call of God in Christ Jesus" (Philippians 3:14). Paul had a goal and took action to attain it. One of the things many of us can do is study more. We can read good books and use Bible-study helps. One of my sons has a practice so that the time he has for reading is most productive. He gathers several books and examines them to decide what to read next, so that his reading contributes more to his interests and learning needs.

We can study our Sunday school lessons and be prepared to respond when our teacher asks questions. We can look for other learning opportunities offered by our church. Surprise your preacher by asking him a question about his sermon. He'll be encouraged to find out you were listening.

Let's cooperate with God's effort to help us grow as Christians by studying more.

Notes

WITNESS MORE

"The fruit of the righteous is a tree of life, and he who is wise wins souls" (Proverbs 11:30). God's definition of wisdom is much different from ours. "My brethren, if any among you strays from the truth, and one turns him back, let him know that he who turns a sinner from the error of his way will save his soul from death, and will cover a multitude of sins" (James 5:19–20).

Only in eternity will we know the good that's done when a person is brought to Christ. Only then will we know how our life has blessed others. "Go therefore and make disciples of all the nations, baptizing them in the name of the Father and the Son and the Holy Spirit" (Matthew 28:19). As you go—as you go about town, as you go wherever you go—tell those you have contact with about the Savior who loves them. Live a life that gives validity to your witness.

"You shall be my witnesses both in Jerusalem, and in all Judea and Samaria, and even to the remotest part of the earth" (Acts 1:8b). Our Jerusalem is the community where we live. There we can have a personal witness. We do the rest through our money, our prayers, and our missionaries. "I have become all things to all men, that I may by all means save some" (1 Corinthians 9:22b). Paul adapted his witness to better relate to each lost person with whom he came in contact.

Jim, in his salvation testimony, said of one person, "He backed me into a corner and tried to compel me to trust Jesus. This other person just brought me some books." Jim watched many professional sports, and the books brought to him had the Christian testimony of some famous athletes. This visitor enabled these athletes to witness to Jim. Jim read the books because they related to his interest. The athletes' Christian testimony led him to trust Christ for salvation.

"Brethren, my heart's desire and my prayer to God for them is for their salvation" (Romans 10:1). Real concern for the lost will help us overcome our timidity and fear of witnessing.

Our witness may be coupled with those of other people who have shared their testimony with the lost person. Some people require a long time and the witness of many others before they can be brought to Christ. Let us pray that our testimony will be involved in others coming to know our Savior.

Remember! There is more than one way to witness, and we need to ask the Lord to help us find the way that is most effective for us.

Every lost person has interests and needs. We need to take time to discover what these are and do our best to cultivate a friendship with the lost person. Ideally, we will then be able to witness more and witness more effectively.

Notes

MOTHER'S DAY

I was middle aged before I discovered that my mother, Ellen Taylor Mee, knew the name of just about every flower, plant, and tree.

I remember how she could play the piano, and I enjoyed hearing her play "The Flight of the Bumblebee."

One of my most vivid memories is of watching my mother pick pears during the Depression, in the 1930s. It was hard work in hot weather, climbing the ladder with a big canvas bag around her neck. She would fill the bag with pears, then climb down the ladder, unhook the bag, and empty the pears into a lug box. She would repeat this all day long. At my mother's funeral, one of her friends told me she had never heard my mother say a bad word about anyone.

Recently a cousin sent me a poem his mother had written about her mother, our grandmother. My cousin's mother was my aunt Margaret, whose birthday was the same as mine. One year I had forgotten my birthday until Aunt Margaret came walking down the road with a cake for me. Here is the poem my aunt Margaret wrote about Effie Mee, my grandmother. (Grandma Mee had four daughters and five sons. Her oldest son was Charles, my father.)

I remember our dear mother how; she woke up every day with a smile, so bright and sunny, for each one along the way.

Always happy, humming softly, always fussing with her flowers. Or just digging in the garden where she worked for endless hours.

And, yet I feel for certain sure; it cannot be denied that she is still there working over on the other side.

I see her, as she used to look, with such a jaunty air; a flower tucked gaily in her hat, her face so sweet and fair.

Always sewing, or a baking; how those little traits we loved, bet she's still as busy as a bee, up there in heaven above.

Yes; I'm sure that on this very day her blue eyes are all aglow, and her arms are filled with flowers as she looks on us below.

And when our trials are over, when we reach the other side, she'll be waiting there to greet us, just beyond the great divide.

There'll be no more tearful partings, no more sad good-byes, where everything is perfect, in God's mansions in the skies.

One day when I was witnessing to my ninety-two-year-old uncle Frank, he said, "I can still remember hearing my mother [Effie Mee] singing, 'And He walks with me and He talks with me and He tells me I am His own.'"

My grandmother was still bearing witness to her Savior many years after she had passed on to be with Him.

Notes

THANKSGIVING

Some form of the word *thanks* appears in the Bible about 160 times. Here are a few of the verses that explain for what and how we are to express our thanksgiving.

"Oh give *thanks* to the Lord, call upon His name; Make known His deeds among the peoples" (Psalm 105:1). Be thankful for all the good things God is doing for us.

"Give *thanks* to the Lord, for He is good; for His loving-kindness is everlasting" (Psalm 118:1). Be thankful for God's goodness and kindness toward us.

"And there must be no filthiness and silly talk, or coarse jesting, but rather giving of *thanks*" (Ephesians 5:4). No idle talk; only expressions of thanksgiving.

"Be anxious for nothing, but in everything by prayer and supplication with *thanksgiving* let your requests be made known to God" (Philippians 4:6). Don't worry, ask God, and give thanks.

"Giving *thanks* to the Father, who has qualified us to share in the inheritance of the saints in light" (Colossians 1:12). Be grateful for our inheritance in Christ.

"As you therefore have received Christ Jesus as Lord, so walk in Him, having been firmly rooted and established in your faith, just as you were instructed and overflowing with *gratitude*" (Colossians 2:6–7).

"And let the peace of Christ rule in your hearts, to which indeed you were called in one body; and be *thankful*" (Colossians 3:15).

"And whatever you do in word or deed, do all in the name of the Lord Jesus, giving *thanks* through Him to the Father" (Colossians 3:17).

"Devote yourselves to prayer, keeping alert in it with an attitude of *thanksgiving*" (Colossians 4:2). May expressions of thanks be on the tips of our tongues.

"In everything give *thanks*; for this is God's will for you in Christ Jesus" (1 Thessalonians 5:18). Not *for everything* but *in everything*.

"First of all, then, I urge that entreaties and prayers, petitions and *thanksgiving*, be made on behalf of all men" (1Timothy 2:1). This may be why my father asked why a person who led in prayer in my Sunday school class didn't pray for the whole world.

"Through Him then, let us continually offer up a sacrifice of praise to God, that is, the fruit of lips that give *thanks* to His name" (Hebrews 13:15). Praise God from whom all blessings flow.

C. S. Lewis said, "We ought to give *thanks* for all fortune: if it is 'good,' because it is good, "if bad' because it works in us patience, humility and the contempt of this world and the hope of our eternal country."[28]

"Be Thankful"[29]

Be thankful for life's simple things
We take for granted every day:
For health and energy to work,
To laugh and love, to sing and play,
For friends and loved ones who stand by
To comfort when we suffer pain,
For God who tenderly restores
Us back to life and health again.

Notes

BIBLE THOUGHTS FOR THE NEW YEAR

"Whatever you do, do your work heartily, as for the Lord rather than for men; knowing that from the Lord you will receive the reward of the inheritance. It is the Lord Christ whom you serve" (Colossians 3:23–24). The Williams translation says "do it with all your heart." The Philips translation reads, "Put your whole heart and soul into it." The Weymouth translation puts it this way: "Let your hearts be in your work."

"Whatever your hand finds to do, verily, do it with all your might" (Ecclesiastes 9:10a). One of my pastors used to put his hands around a child's throat and quote that verse. The child probably memorized it quickly.

What work shall we do with such enthusiasm? We should do what Jesus came to do. Jesus said to Peter, "I will build my church; and the gates of Hades shall not overpower it" (Matthew 16:18). This tells us that we should be zealously working to enlarge and strengthen our church and the mission work our church supports.

Most of us can quote this verse: "Go therefore and make disciples of all the nations, baptizing them in the name of the Father and the Son and the Holy Spirit, teaching them to observe all that I commanded you; and lo, I am with you always, even to the end of the age" (Matthew 28:19–20). What Jesus said is very clear. We should be doing what He commanded. Someone observed, "No go, no lo."

We are told that God has given us "pastors and teachers for the equipping of the saints for the work of service, to the building up of the body of Christ" (Ephesians 4:11b–12). We also learn in Ephesians that "He put all things in subjection under His feet, and gave Him as head over all things to the church, which is His body, the fullness of Him who fills all in all" (Ephesians 1:22–23). All of the above tell us that we should be working enthusiastically to strengthen and build up our churches, which, with other churches, represent the body of Christ in this world.

The Bible verses listed above challenge us to make a greater commitment to God's work through our churches by being faithful in attendance, diligent in our service, and generous in our financial support.

The Bible is clear about how we should do our service for the Lord: "Whatever you do, do your work heartily, as for the Lord rather than for men; knowing that from the Lord you will receive the reward of the inheritance. It is the Lord Christ whom you serve" (Colossians 3:23–24). We need to keep our focus on whom we serve. It is hard to remember that we serve the Lord rather than the people around us or over us.

> The church's one foundation is Jesus Christ her Lord;[30]
> She is His new creation, by Spirit and the Word:
> From heaven He came and sought her to be His holy bride,
> With His own blood He bought her, and for her life He died.

Notes

Do Less

For one New Year's resolution I used the theme "*Do More.*" I considered just repeating that theme for the next New Year. Then it occurred to me that a good theme would be "*Do Less.*" As with all suggestions I would say, "If the shoe fits, wear it."

Some of us may need to *eat less.* I have been trying for a couple of years to get my weight down below 190. I lose a few pounds and then gain them right back. "The glutton will come to poverty" (Proverbs 23:21). I don't consider myself a glutton, but in contrast with how little some people eat, I may be. I know that one of the diet recommendations is to eat smaller portions. That is hard to do when you have a wife who cooks like mine.

My hygiene teacher at Medford High, in Oregon, was Bill Bowerman, who later became the major owner of Nike. I remember him saying that "We should eat one serving or one plateful and then pull back from the table."

Then we should *worry less.* Matthew 6:31 says, in part, "Do not be anxious." Worry can cause ulcers and shows a lack of faith in our heavenly Father. I daresay that nearly all of the bad things we were afraid were going to happen didn't occur. Jesus rebuked Martha: "Martha, Martha, you are worried and bothered about so many things; but only a few things are necessary, really only one, for Mary has chosen the good part, which shall not be taken from her" (Luke 10:41–42). Mary was giving her attention to Jesus while Martha was "distracted with all her preparations."

And then let's *complain less.* Worry is fear that something bad is going to happen, whereas complaining is fussing because something is being done differently from what we would prefer or something is not being done that we think should be. Now, we may be correct in our concern, but complaining about it to someone who can't do anything about it won't accomplish anything.

"Do not complain, brethren, against one another, that yourselves may not be judged; behold, the judge is standing right at the door" (James 5:9). When we have a complaint, we need to find out who is involved and talk to them about it. Many times we will find we didn't have all the facts or that someone gave us the wrong information.

I thought of a few more possibilities such as *criticize less,* *"brag less,* or *gossip less.* But then, we aren't supposed to do these at all.

We will do well if we eat less, worry less, and complain less. I think we'll be happier and more content, and the people around us will be very appreciative.

Notes

God's Christmas Gift

"For the wages of sin is death, but the free gift of God is eternal life in Christ Jesus our Lord" (Romans 6:23). "Therefore having been justified by faith, we have peace with God through our Lord Jesus Christ, through whom also we have obtained our introduction by faith into this grace in which we stand; and we exult in hope of the glory of God" (Romans 5:1–2).

"How blessed is he whose transgression is forgiven, whose sin is covered" (Psalm 32:1). "Blessed are those whose lawless deeds have been forgiven, and whose sins have been covered. Blessed is the man whose sin the Lord will not take into account" (Romans 4:7–8). "He made Him who knew no sin to be sin on our behalf, that we might become the righteousness of God in Him" (2 Corinthians 5:21).

What is the gift that we receive through our faith in Jesus Christ? Eternal life, yes! Eternal life begins at conversion. Peace, yes! A genuine peace that nothing else in the world can give and no one can take away. Blessed, made happy in Jesus, yes!

What is the gift that makes all the other gifts a reality? One clue is that God has gotten our sin out of the way. "As far as the east is from the west, so far has He removed our transgressions from us" (Psalm 103:12).

This was necessary because God cannot fellowship with sin. Sin separates us from God. Our sin creates a great gulf between us and God. God made a bridge over that gulf. That bridge is Jesus' death on the cross or literally the shedding of His blood. "In Him we have redemption through His blood, the forgiveness of our trespasses, according to the riches of His grace" (Ephesians 1:7). "And according to the law, one may almost say, all things are cleansed with blood, and without shedding of blood there is no forgiveness" (Hebrews 9:22).

Blood is mentioned in the Bible more than 300 times. "For the life of the flesh is in the blood" (Leviticus 17:11a). Much of the mention of blood in the Bible alludes directly or indirectly to Jesus' blood, shed on the cross to make possible our salvation.

So how is it possible that God looks at us now and doesn't see our sin? Our sin is now out of the way. It no longer comes between us and our Creator, who has now become our heavenly Father.

It is explained in 2 Corinthians 5:21, which we read earlier. "We become the righteousness of God in Him."

Here is the gift, the gift that bridges the chasm between us and God. The gift makes possible a close relationship with God. It is the gift that enables us to call out to God as "Daddy," saying "Abba Father" and to call Jesus our brother and makes heaven our future home.

It is the gift of Jesus' sinless life, the righteousness of Christ that is given us at conversion and that God now sees when He looks at us.

Notes

JESUS IS ALIVE

The psalmist said, "For you will not abandon me to Sheol; You will not allow Your Faithful One to see decay" (Psalm 16:10, HCSB). True to this prophecy, on the Sunday morning after His crucifixion, the stone had been rolled away and the tomb was empty. Jesus, on that day, walked with two men on the road to Emmaus.

At a gathering of the disciples, who were talking about what had happened, Jesus suddenly appeared. Apparently, He had walked through a solid wall. Won't that be something when one day we will have a body like His resurrected body?

Not only is Jesus alive, at the right hand of the Father in heaven, but He is busy working for His own. "He is always able to save those who come to God through Him, since He always lives to intercede for them" (Hebrews 7:25, HCSB). He is alive serving as our High Priest. He has made it possible for us to approach our heavenly Father to make our request known to Him. What a blessing it is to know that the Creator of the universe, the one who made us, is alive and working on our behalf.

He has given us responsibility. Our job is to introduce Him to those who don't know Him. We are to live in a way that shows He is alive in us. Jesus is busy building His church, of which He is the head. What an encouragement it is to realize that our seventy, eighty, or ninety years in this life is not all there is. It is exciting to anticipate a future with our Lord, but none of this would be true if Jesus were still in the tomb where they laid Him.

Jesus' resurrection is the cornerstone of our faith. Without the resurrection, we would have no hope of a future in heaven. Paul explains this: "If there is no resurrection of the dead, then Christ has not been raised." Paul goes on to say, "And if Christ be not raised, your faith is worthless; you are still in your sins." Paul declares, "But now Christ has been raised from the dead, the first fruits of those who have fallen asleep" (1 Corinthians 15:13, 17, 20, HCSB). Our faith in Christ is dependent on His resurrection.

Christianity is the only religion that has a living savior. The empty tomb is unique to our faith. Let's be busy sharing this truth with others. Polls indicate that a large majority of Americans believe there is a God. 92% answered yes to the question, "Do you believe in God" in a gallop poll taken May 5 – 8, 2011.[31] It would be interesting to know how many believe in the resurrection.

Believing in the resurrection is vital to being saved. "If you confess with your mouth, Jesus is Lord, and believe in your heart that God raised Him from the dead, you will be saved" (Romans 10:9, HCSB).

May each Easter season increase our faith and give us a greater appreciation for the reality and importance of Jesus' resurrection.

Notes

Through God's Eyes

Death[32]

These thoughts are taken from the book *Through God's Eyes* by Harold E. Dye. The author, with Pablo his guide, went to an Arizona desert to convalesce from a heart problem. Their first experience was seeing a night-blooming flower. It was very beautiful with a sweet aroma, but lived only one night and then died. Why it lived only one night puzzled Pablo, and he blurted out, "If I were God ..." *If I were God* became the theme for the rest of their desert experience.

The desert showed many evidences of death, with dried bones and broken wagon wheels. Water holes were eighty miles apart. Harold Dye thought about death. Finally, the author declared, "If I were God, I would abolish death."

Then he began to think of the consequences of such an act. Chaos would at one stroke be brought to civilization. Trends of progress would be stopped forever. If a man did not know that he would surely die, he would sit still forever, stagnating and decaying. Man's limited time prompts him to invent time-saving devices, compose beautiful music, and write books and poetry. One of the deepest instincts of the race is self-perpetuation through procreation. Men desire to live on through the lives of their children.

It is primarily because a man knows that he will die that he has religion in his heart and life. There would be no churches were it not for the shadow of death. It is because of the presence of death in the world that Jesus established His church—to safeguard the way of eternal life. Christ died that man might fear death no longer and might rather welcome it as the entrance to that more joyous life beyond the shores of time.

"There comes a time—a precious hour—when the Christian finally lays down his burned-out body in the last dreamless, peaceful sleep. Earth's scenes grow dim. One like unto the Son of Man leaves the open door of heaven and walks with outstretched hand in welcome. Then, at last, rest comes to the child of God. He leaves the land in which he was never at home, where he was a stranger and a pilgrim, and enters upon his inheritance, the place Jesus has prepared for him. Here is Dye's concluding statement about death,

> "Death is not our enemy! 'If I were God, I would do away with death.' I echoed the cry of Pablo that night as we watched the fading of a rare desert flower which had lived its tiny moment of glory only to fade forever. 'I am God in Christ!' shouts the voice of Infinity, and 'I have ABOLISHED DEATH FOREVER FOR THOSE WHO TRUST IN ME'". "And He shall wipe away every tear from their eyes; and there shall no longer be any death; there shall no longer be any mourning, or crying, or pain; the first things have passed away" (Revelation 21:4).[33]

Notes

PAIN[34]

Harold Dye, author of *Through God's Eyes,* notes as they continued their desert trip that his friend Pablo was tugging at his pants where sharp cactus needles were sticking into his leg. He describes how the desert was covered with symbols of pain. Nearly every plant was tipped with bloodletting needles of torture. Then there were horned lizards, porcupines, gila monsters, tarantula wasps, and coyotes with razor like teeth. All this made him conscious of the vexing riddle of pain.

It seemed incongruous with a good, loving God. We have lived with pain since Eden. If we could hear the centuries of history, our ears would be bombarded with the crying, groaning, wailing, shrieking, and screaming of suffering humanity.

Many artists, theologians, explorers, and leaders did their thing in spite of and perhaps because of their pain. Columbus was stricken with a bad attack of gout on the high seas while making his third voyage to the West Indies. Martin Luther suffered from gout, and at Wartburg and Smalkald, where he was fighting on behalf of freedom of conscience, his work was hampered by gravel, headache, and earache.

John Calvin had such violent migraines that when they came on, he could scarcely speak. Louis Pasteur was partially paralyzed and with this handicap fought almost constant pain as he bent over his animals and test tubes.

The author said to Pablo, "Do you not see any good in pain? Pablo responded, "Oh yes, pain is good for someone I do not like."

Then the author began to think of what the consequences would be if God never allowed pain. The primary function of pain is biological. The brain has twelve billion cells that tell us of pain in or on any part of our body, without which we would soon die. We could put our hand on a hot stove and not feel it. Pain is like a smoke alarm that lets us know when we have a problem.

Pain has a spiritual significance in that it has caused countless people to look to God. Paul speaks of the "fellowship of His suffering." "That I may know Him, and the power of His resurrection and the fellowship of His sufferings, being conformed to His death" (Philippians 3:10). Jesus suffered agonizing pain on our behalf. God forbid that we should falter in our faith over pain.

Jesus is aware of our pain. "Since then we have a great high priest who has passed through the heavens, Jesus the Son of God, let us hold fast our confession. For we do not have a high priest who cannot sympathize with our weaknesses, but one who has been tempted in all things as we are, yet without sin" (Hebrews 4:14–15).

Jesus suffered agonizing pain to secure our forgiveness for sin and a place in heaven, where we are told in Revelation 21:4, *there will be no more pain.*

Notes

POVERTY[35]

In *Through God's Eyes* author Harold Dye says, "Before us, all around us the alkali sands stretched, broken here and there by rude desert growth, but barren, cheerless, dismal and suffocating. They seemed to speak of human poverty: blind, crushing, blighting, blistering, searing poverty that robs life of beauty, hearts of their hope, and eyes of their dreams."

Who can watch bread lines, with spiritless, dirty-faced, ragged, wretched human beings and not long for the power of God to rid the Earth of such scenes? Should God destroy poverty? If He did, He at one stroke would become not a benefactor but a taskmaster. Man's will would have been erased, without which, no matter how great his earthly riches, man would be infinitely poor.

Poverty serves a purpose in human development. No Handel labored in a glittering conservatory. No Bunyan wore diamonds. No Einstein was reared on marble floors. No Gandhi ever fingered stocks and bonds.

Jesus declared that it is impossible for a rich man to enter heaven. Fortunately, all things are possible with God. Wealth without integrity produces unbounded evil. Poverty becomes a test of character. We have the right to earthly possessions if we can obtain them intelligently, industriously, and honestly.

Pharaoh was poor though materially rich, whereas Moses was rich though materially poor. Nero was poor though rich with Rome's wealth, whereas Paul was rich while lying in a Roman jail. Pilate was poor, though his palace was of marble, whereas Jesus was rich but had nowhere to lay his head."

Wealth does not provide the depth of satisfaction and happiness to be found in family and friends. These are values that many have lost as they have become rich.

Tom Brokaw wrote a book called *The Greatest Generation,* about the generation that came through the Great Depression, which started after the stock market crashed in 1929. The Depression taught us about thrift and hard work. My family weathered the Great Depression through hard work and doing without some luxuries. My parents worked during the fruit-harvesting seasons. It was tough on my mother, climbing a long ladder with a bag of pears around her neck. My dad sold Christmas trees standing in the cold on a street corner in Medford, Oregon. We were happy and never went hungry.

Jesus says, "The poor you have with you always" (Matthew 16:11). The Bible says, "God chose the poor of this world to be rich in faith" (James 2:5). There are many poor people who are happy because they know Jesus as Savior.

There are many rich people who are miserable because they are lost in their sin and don't look to God and His Word for help with life's decisions and problems.

Notes

Evil[36]

Part of this material is taken from *Through God's Eyes* by Harold Dye and part from my own experience. As Pablo and Dye continued their time in the desert, Pablo heard a rattlesnake and tumbled backward with a cry of fright. Though this chapter begins with a rattlesnake, the author's discussion doesn't imply that snakes and other poisonous creatures are evil.

One summer when I was just a boy, my family camped out at Lake of the Woods in southern Oregon. My father was foreman of a crew that was building a lookout station on top of one of the mountains. One evening I was walking on a path near the camp when I heard a rattlesnake. I hurried back to get one of the crew members and showed him where I had heard the snake. The worker found the snake, and with a forked stick, he dragged it out onto the path. Holding the snake with the stick, he spit tobacco juice into the snake's mouth, and in less than a minute the snake was stone dead.

Is a poisonous snake evil? Snakebites are bad, but are snakes, mosquitoes, black widow spiders, and other such creatures evil? I think not. They just do what comes naturally for them. They do not have free will.

Satan is depicted as a snake in the Garden of Eden, where he tempted Eve to disobey God. That is where sin originated.

Dye asks, "Why did God create man, knowing that he would fall? Is God the author of evil? Does sin serve any purpose in the life of man? To that last query, which seems to sum up all the rest, we would unhesitatingly say that the free will to sin or not to sin ultimately lifts man from the role of creature to that of son of God.

If the power to sin were taken away, the power of will would be an absurdity. Because man did sin, and fall, he became eligible to be born again—to become the child of God through faith in Christ Jesus—born, not made. God is the father of all men in a creative sense, not in a spiritual. Men belong to the family of God only as they become brothers in Christ."

God did not want a horde of goose-stepping mechanical beings having no volition of their own; He wanted sons and daughters, begotten of Him through love.

Dye continues: "One day the Master stooped and made a man and breathed into his nostrils the breath of life, and the man became a living spirit. One day the man and his wife fell into sin, but God made a way of escape for the federal head of the human race and for all men to follow. That way of escape was by substituting the death of the sinless, only begotten Son of God upon the cross. And the sinner, repenting and turning from his sin to accept Christ into his heart through faith, looks up into the eyes of God and says, 'I love thee, Father.' He knows why he loves.

If I were God, I would do away with sin, Well, now, that is exactly what God has done. He has done away with the power of sin to bind, to damn, and to kill forever for those who have no condemnation, who are in Christ Jesus."

Dye concludes the chapter with this statement: "There will be no sin in heaven."

Notes

GOD AND JESUS

GOD'S WILL

The word *will* appears 7,582 times in the Bible. I found a reference to *God's will* or *His will* thirty times in the New Testament. I could not find a reference to *God's will* in the Old Testament. In the Old Testament there are hundreds of statements where God says, "I will." In the New Testament there are no statements where God says, "I will." There are only a few times where Jesus says, "I will"—such as "I will make you fishers of men."

Finding God's will for one's life and throughout life is a much-discussed subject. We have heard people declare, "It was God's will" about things that have happened to them. I have heard testimonies about how a person decided it was God's will that the person chose a particular profession. Nearly all ministers say that God called them into the ministry.

My own experience was that God wanted me in full-time Christian service. I interpreted it in the beginning that God wanted me in a profession that involved people more than in one that would have involved mechanical engineering. I didn't know much about positions in church work, so I decided on public education.

I was preparing to be a principal or a superintendent. I taught school for three years while working on my master's degree in education. Just before my last semester of graduate study, I still had a feeling I needed to be in something different. Our church had a study of *Every Christian's Job* by C. E. Matthews, and during that study I concluded that God wanted me in full-time Christian service. I made it public, and the feeling that I needed to do something else disappeared and never returned.

Immanuel Baptist Church asked me to be their minister of education, which I was for eight years. Then Wayne Todd, who was my pastor for four of the eight years, went to the Baptist Sunday School Board as secretary of the Library Service. He asked me to come be supervisor of the Field Services section. I retired from that position after thirty years in 1990. The feeling never returned that I needed to be in some other line of work.

I have heard others give their testimony, and nearly everyone said that they had had an undercurrent of feeling that wouldn't go away until they decided it was God's call and they yielded to it.

Deciding on a life's work is one thing, but knowing God's will in every aspect of life is quite another need. You have heard it said that "the center of God's will is the safest place in the world." The only genuine happiness is to know and do God's will. Paul said to one group, "So that I may come to you in joy by the will of God and find refreshing rest in your company" (Romans 15:32).

The Lord's Prayer reads, "Thy kingdom come, Thy will be done, on earth as it is in heaven" (Matthew 6:10).

Notes

God's Will No. 2

In another devotional on this same topic, we looked at the number of times *will of God* appeared in the Bible. A concordance for the New American Standard Bible lists the word *will* 7,582 times.

We also found that there was no word in Hebrew for the concept of the "will of God." According to the *Interpreter's Dictionary of the Bible,* the Old Testament uses words such as *purpose, favor, grace,* and *delight* to express "God's will." Here is an example: "The sacrifice of the wicked is and abomination to the Lord but the prayer of the upright is His delight" (Proverbs 15:8).

An example of the word *purpose*: "Declaring the end from the beginning and from ancient times things which have not been, saying, My purpose will be established, and I will accomplish all my good pleasure" (Isaiah 46:10). This reminded me of a verse in Revelation: "Thou art worthy O Lord, to receive glory and honor and power: for thou hast created all things, and for Thy **pleasure** they are and were created." (Revelation 4:11, KJV). The New American Standard Bible reads "and because of **Thy will** they existed and were created."

The use of the word *pleasure,* instead of *will,* in the King James Version may explain why when I checked the use of the word *will* in *Cruden's Exhaustive Concordance,* which is based on the King James Bible, the word *will* occurred only 3,746 times. It is an example of how language has changed since the 1600s, when the King James translation was done.

So what does the New Testament say about the "will of God"? Jesus said, "For this is the will of My Father, that everyone who beholds the Son, and believes in Him, may have eternal life; and I Myself will raise him up on the last day" (John 6:40). What a great promise that this life is not all there is.

Paul tells us to "not be conformed to this world, but be transformed by the renewing of your mind, that you may prove what the will of God is, that which is good and acceptable and perfect" (Romans 12:2). It is God's will that we know what is good and acceptable and perfect. Peter adds, "That such is the will of God that by doing right you might silence the ignorance of foolish men. Act as free men, and do not use your freedom as a covering for evil, but use is as bond slaves of God" (1 Peter 2:15–16). We have great freedom in Christ, but Peter tells us not to abuse it.

First Thessalonians tells us how to live: "Rejoice always; pray without ceasing; in everything give thanks; for this is God's will for you in Christ Jesus" (5:16–18). Sailors use the stars to get their bearings and to stay on course. The Bible tells us how to stay on course. The right course is living according to God's will.

Notes

God at Work

It is good to know that God is at work for us, in us, and through us. The Bible has a lot to say about work, working, works, workmen, and workers. In some form, *work* appears in the Bible almost 600 times.

First there is the start of everything: "In the beginning God created the heavens and the earth" (Genesis 1:1). Later we read, "Then God said, Let us make man in our image" (Genesis 1:26). Sometime later God realized that man needed a mate: "Then the Lord God said it is not good for man to be alone; I will make him a helper suitable for him" (Genesis 2:18).

Later Adam and Eve sinned, and God covered them with skins of an animal. This was symbolic in that the animal's blood had to be shed to provide the skins. God was the first seamstress: "And the Lord God made garments of skin for Adam and his wife and God clothed them" (Genesis 3:21).

Sometime later we find that God is an author. "And the tablets were God's work, and the writing was God's writing engraved on the tablets" (Exodus 32:16). Jesus came to do God's work. "Jesus said to them, My food is to do the will of Him who sent Me, and to accomplish His work" (John 4:34).

God was a manager who delegated His work to His son Jesus. Of course this is hard for us to understand since Jesus is God. People were asking, "'what shall we do that we may work the works of God?' Jesus answered and said to them, 'This is the work of God that you believe in Him whom He has sent'" (John 6:28–29). God's main work on earth now is to bring men to Himself through His Son Jesus.

God is interested in our welfare: "God causes all things to work together for good to those who love God, to those who are called according to His purpose" (Romans 8:28). Sometimes some of the things that happen to us don't seem so good. If we are patient and wait before passing judgment, we will discover that God has worked good in us or through us.

Of course God doesn't do this for everyone. Loving God and being called are serious conditions. Also, what is good in God's sight is explained in verse 29: "For whom He foreknew, He also predestined to become conformed to the image of His Son, that He might be the first-born among many brethren" (Romans 8:29). In God's sight good is that which causes us to become more like Jesus. Good comes from our contact with others when we are able to minister to them because of the hard things that happened to us.

God is persistent in this work: "For I am confident of this very thing, that He who began a good work in you will perfect it until the day of Jesus Christ" (Philippians 1:6). One of my favorite Scriptures is "So then, my beloved, just as you have always obeyed, not as in my presence only, but now much more in my absence, work out your salvation with fear and trembling; for it is God who is at work in you, both to will and to work for His good pleasure" (Philippians 2:12–13). God is at work in us, shaping us in the image of Christ. What He needs is our wholehearted cooperation.

"But we all, with unveiled face beholding as in a mirror the glory of the Lord, are being transformed into the same image from glory to glory, just as from the Lord the Spirit" (2 Corinthians 3:18).

God really is at work in us, for us, and through us to help us be more like Jesus and to help others come to know our wonderful Savior, Jesus Christ.

Notes

As You Go

"Go therefore and make disciples of all the nations" (Matthew 28:19a). "But you shall receive power when the Holy Spirit has come upon you; and you shall be my witnesses both in Jerusalem, and in all Judea and Samaria, and even to the remotest part of the earth" (Acts 1:8). We never retire from this commission or grow so old that Jesus' words don't apply to us. A retired minister has been a living example of this. For twenty years he and his wife have faithfully visited the sick, the shut-ins, and people in nursing homes.

Some senior adults may still go on brief mission trips, but most of them no longer go beyond their community. No one ever grows too old to support Jesus' Great Commission. Everyone can still witness to their neighbors, their family members, relatives, and others with whom they come into contact in stores and other places.

Then there is prayer. *Open Windows,* a devotional publication, lists the missionaries who have birthdays on the date of each reading. These are missionaries for the Southern Baptist International Mission Board and the North American Mission Board. In sensitive areas where the missionaries might be in danger, only their initials are given. There are about 5,000 missionaries for each of the home and foreign boards, or a total of about 10,000. We can pray for them day by day.

Then we can give. Each fall Southern Baptists are encouraged to give to the Lottie Moon Offering, which is the Southern Baptist foreign mission offering. The North American Mission Board has the Annie Armstrong Offering, which is given in the spring. We can minister and witness to people in our own area, and we can pray and give to support others who go.

In 1953 Wayne Todd came to be the pastor of the Immanuel Baptist Church in Lexington, Kentucky, where I was minister of education. That Christmas, under his leadership, we started the Christmas for Christ offering. The challenge was to give as much to the Christmas missions offering as we spent on gifts for family and friends. We were to give generous gifts to Christ on His birthday. Immanuel has continued that practice, resulting in significant money for missions.

Jesus was the ultimate missionary. He came all the way from heaven to save us from our sin. He showed us the way as He walked about the countryside, teaching and healing. He quoted the Old Testament and sent His disciples on missionary outings. We have the whole Bible to guide us and to quote. He challenges us to go and share it with the lost in our neighborhood and around the world through giving, going, and praying.

Notes

FREEDOM IN CHRIST

"For you were called to freedom, brethren; only do not turn your freedom into an opportunity for the flesh, but through love serve one another" (Galatians 5:13). Paul says, "All things are lawful for me, but not all things are profitable. All things are lawful for me but I will not be mastered by anything" (1 Corinthians 6:12).

Probably most of us, when we were first saved, went through the process of deciding, as a Christian, what we could and should not do.

What was legal seemed to vary with the denominations. I remember one person who switched churches so it would be all right for him to drink beer or wine. Out West, Christians weren't supposed to smoke. A church in Richmond, Virginia, had ashtrays in the church parlor.

We don't live on an island where we have no influence on other people, and the Scripture is very clear that what we give ourselves permission to do ought to be decided by how it would influence other people, especially weaker or young Christians and the unsaved. As Paul said, "All things are lawful but all are not profitable." Paul gives us some help in deciding what is okay for the Christian. "I know and am convinced in the Lord Jesus that nothing is unclean in itself; but to him who thinks anything to be unclean, to him it is unclean" (Romans 14:14). If we think something is wrong and we do it anyway, it is sinful.

Another way of thinking about it is this: "The faith which you have, have as your own conviction before God. Happy is he who does not condemn himself in what he approves. But he who doubts is condemned if he eats, because his eating is not from faith; and whatever is not from faith is sin" (Romans 14:22–23).

Paul had been discussing the eating of meat that had been sacrificed to idols. He gave two guidelines: First, the effect our actions have on weaker Christians. Verse 21 says, "It is good not to eat meat or to drink wine, or to do anything by which your brother stumbles." We have freedom as Christians, but because of our influence on others, we have to do what has a positive influence on one another. This covers more than things we should not do. Church attendance, stewardship, and service also have an effect on our neighbors, family, and fellow church members. Our faithful attendance and the way we serve in our church will influence those around us. Second, if we don't have faith that God approves, we should avoid it.

Finally, here is a way to summarize how our life in Christ should be lived: "So then let us pursue the things which make for peace and the building up of one another" (Romans 14:19).

We have great freedom as Christians, but we cannot allow our freedom to stand in the way of lost people finding Christ. Neither can we allow our freedom to be a stumbling block for weaker Christians. The major guideline for us is Christian love, which requires us to always do that which is in the best interests of the other person.

Notes

His Name

Think of it! Jesus was named hundreds of years before He was born. "For a child will be born to us, a son will be given to us; and the government will rest upon His shoulders; And His name will be called Wonderful Counselor, Mighty God, Eternal Father, Prince of Peace. There will be no end to the increase of His government or of peace, on the throne of David and over His kingdom, to establish it and to uphold it with justice and righteousness from then on and forevermore. The zeal of the Lord of hosts will accomplish this" (Isaiah 9:6–7).

Who else in all of history was not only predicted but named centuries before He arrived on Earth. From the very beginning of time He was foretold. In Genesis 3 we are told that because the first humans were misled by Satan and disobeyed their creator, God said He (Jesus) will bruise you (Satan) on the head and you will bruise Him (Jesus) on the heel. The crucifixion did bruise Jesus, but because of the cross, Satan's ultimate doom was sealed and His free rein over mankind was greatly reduced.

Even Jesus' virgin birth was prophesied. In the Genesis account He was referred to as *her seed.* Isaiah told us, "Therefore the Lord Himself will give you a sign: Behold, a virgin will be with child and bear a son, and she will call His name Immanuel" (Isaiah 7:14).

In Luke's gospel we are told that Gabriel came to Mary and told her, "Hail favored one! The Lord is with you. Behold you will conceive in your womb, and bear a son, and you shall name Him Jesus" (Luke 1:28, 31). Gabriel went on to say, "His kingdom will have no end." As we celebrate Jesus' birth another time, how about Jesus' reign in His kingdom?

His reign in the hearts of humankind spans the Earth. There are Christians in every nation on Earth. Jesus said, "I will build my church." The 2011 Yearbook of American and Canadian Churches reported more than 30 million members in the eight Baptist conventions that had more than one million members each. More than half the Baptists were in the Southern Baptist Convention which reported 16.3 million members.

Jesus reigns in the hearts of men. He truly is the Prince of Peace and a Wonderful Counselor. All who have received Him as Savior can have a peace that truly is beyond understanding. And everyone who heeds His advice finds that He really is a Wonderful Counselor. His reign is in our hearts, and His kingdom grows as more turn to Him for salvation.

Many churches collect money for missions during the Christmas season. This is appropriate, since we observe Christmas as His birthday. Christmas offerings that support missions around the world will result in many coming to know our Savior. How could any other Christmas gift be more meaningful than that?

Notes

Jesus the Carpenter

One night I dreamed I was in a meeting with some preachers. In the dream, I handed one of the preachers a book that apparently had to do with Jesus as a carpenter. The preacher made some negative remark about the carpenter part as though it had no theological or scriptural significance.

I was awakened and lay there thinking about the dream. It occurred to me that there had to be something of importance in the fact that our Savior started out as a carpenter. He grew up in the home of his father, Joseph, who was a carpenter. I got out of bed and made some notes, because dreams can vanish in the twinkling of an eye, and I thought this one ought to be remembered.

My dad was a carpenter and a good one. One of his homes got recognition in a national magazine. My youngest brother was an architect, and he helped with the design of that house, which was built in Oakland, California. My other brother was one of the carpenters on the project. I can remember being around the houses that Dad was building in Medford, Oregon, when I was only eight or nine years old. One day I was hammering away at something and a few seconds after Dad told me I was going to hit my thumb I hit it. I have a scar on my left thumb that reminds me of that experience.

Here are some thoughts that were triggered by my dream. Jesus worked as a carpenter, which enables Him to relate to the vast majority of people in the world who work at all kinds of jobs that provide us homes to live in. Can you think of any other job that would have enabled Him to relate to more people?

Carpentry is a physical job that would have made Him physically strong for His three years of walking around the Holy Land teaching and healing, and finally for the ordeal on the cross.

There are many references in Scripture to the construction of buildings. There are five references by Old Testament prophets to a plumb line. "And the Lord said, to me, 'What do you see, Amos?' And I said, 'A plumb line.' Then the Lord said, 'Behold I am about to put a plumb line in the midst of My people Israel. I will spare them no longer'" (Amos 7:8). Jesus may be our plumb line. A plumb line is used to tell if a wall or a post is perfectly vertical. Jesus lived a perfect life, and every person shows up as imperfect when compared with Him.

Foundation or *foundations* appear in the Bible eighty-one times. Here is one instance: "For no man can lay a foundation other than the one which is laid, which is Jesus Christ" (1 Corinthians 3:11). Our lives need a firm foundation, and there is none better than Jesus and His word the Bible.

Jesus said, "Therefore everyone who hears these words of Mine, and acts upon them, may be compared to a wise man, who built his house upon the rock" (Matthew 7:24). His house held up when the storms came, not like the one who built his house on the sands of man's opinion and philosophy.

Jesus is the master builder of lives. Let Him construct your life.

Notes

The Lord's Prayer

The Prayer

"When you are praying, do not use meaningless repetition, as the Gentiles do, for they suppose that they will be heard for their many words" (Matthew 6:7). This is part of the advice Jesus gave His disciples before giving them the Lord's Prayer. If Jesus were in our midst today, I don't think He would call us Gentiles even though that is what we are. I think He would call us brothers and sisters.

Jesus would give us the same advice about praying that He gave His disciples. He didn't say not to use repetition but not to use meaningless repetition. At times I think I shouldn't be repeating the same prayer requests day after day. Then I realize that praying for my brother to be saved is not meaningless, although it is an often-repeated prayer.

However the Gentiles were praying, Jesus said that His disciples were not to be like them. Then He said that the Father knows what we need before we ask Him. I would conclude that meaningless prayer is praying for things we don't need and repeating it over and over. It is not surprising that God knows what we need. He made us, and He even knows how many hairs we have on our heads.

Jesus told them how they should pray. "Therefore do not be like them; for your Father knows what you need, before you ask Him." He then tells them the words to use (Matthew 6:8–9a).

This is from the King James Version, which is the wording that is familiar to most of us. "Our Father which art in heaven, hallowed be thy name. Thy kingdom come, Thy will be done in earth, as it is in heaven. Give us this day our daily bread, and forgive us our debts as we forgive our debtors. And lead us not into temptation, but deliver us from evil: For Thine is the kingdom, and the power, and the glory, forever. Amen" (Matthew 6:9b–13).

Following the Lord's Prayer is the Lord's admonition about forgiveness, something that is very critical to God. One of the greatest hindrances to unity and fellowship in our churches is the grudges that people hold against each other. For Jesus to say this, after His pattern for prayer, would seem to say that holding grudges, in His estimation, is one of the most serious sins and a great hindrance to our prayer life.

Lack of forgiveness has split churches and destroyed friendships. Scripture says that God doesn't even want our offerings if we know that someone is holding something against us. "If therefore you are presenting your offering at the altar, and there remember that your brother has something against you, leave your offering there before the altar, and go your way; first be reconciled to your brother and then come and present your offering" (Matthew 5:23–24, KJV).

There is more to effective prayer than just opening our mouth and uttering words.

Notes

OUR FATHER

"Our Father who art in heaven, Hallowed be Thy name" (Matthew 6:9). Who can pray this prayer? The answer is that only those who have been saved by the shed blood of God's Son, Jesus Christ, can pray it. These are the only people who can say "our Father." God will not fellowship with people whose sin has not been covered, forgiven, and removed. We are reminded of this truth: "He made Him who knew no sin to be sin on our behalf, that we might become the righteousness of God in Him" (2 Corinthians 5:21).

One way of thinking about this prayer is that Jesus was teaching His disciples how to pray. He was not talking to a crowd in the local community. He was saying this to His disciples, those who had chosen to follow Him. His disciples today are the saved members of His church, the church that Jesus is building. What a glorious privilege it is to be one of that number. The words are *our* Father, not *my* Father; it reminds us that we are part of a great family, the family of God.

When we pray, we are addressing the One who made us. He knows our every need. Those who don't know Him as Father are on their own in a cruel, competitive world. In a sense they are orphans.

Our heavenly Father is in heaven. That is a grand place where all of His children will be one day. Life on this earth can be really dismal when the time comes leave it and the lost person has no hope to be in heaven with the Father.

When we think of our heavenly Father, we are to do so with great respect and reverence. His name is not to be spoken of carelessly or frivolously. The third commandment says, "You shall not take the name of the Lord your God in vain, for the Lord will not leave him unpunished who takes His name in vain" (Exodus 20:7). *Hallowed* means that God's name is different. It is set apart from all others. We are not to treat His name in any careless or thoughtless way. His name is to be revered and honored. "Our father in heaven, Your name be honored as holy" (Matthew 6:9, HCSB).

We have a special privilege as expressed in Romans: "For you have not received a spirit of slavery, leading to fear again, but you have received a spirit of adoption as sons by which we cry out, Abba! Father!" I understand that Abba is akin to *Daddy*.

God is unique. He is special. He is one of a kind. Though we are encouraged to call Him Daddy, He is not one of the gang or a buddy.

His name is to be hallowed, a name that is above every name. He is holy, one set apart and treated with utmost respect.

The very first song in the Baptist Hymnal[37] is "Holy, Holy, Holy." The title for the hymn came from this verse in Isaiah: "Holy, holy, holy is the Lord of Hosts; His glory fills the whole earth" (Isaiah 6:3, HCSB).

Notes

Thy Kingdom Come

"Thy kingdom come. Thy will be done, on earth as it is in heaven" (Matthew 6:10). How does God's kingdom come on earth? First of all, His kingdom is the rule of God in the hearts of men. How does God establish His rule in the hearts of men? Jesus' commission to His followers, before He left this earth, was to "Go and make disciples" (Matthew 28:18). Jesus said to Peter, "I will build my church."

We understand that we are the body and that Jesus is the head. A head depends on the hands and feet and voice of the body to get things done. "Speaking the truth in love, we are to grow up in all aspects into Him who is the head even Christ, from whom the whole body, being fitted and held together by that which every joint supplies, according to the proper working of each individual part, causes the growth of the body for the building up of itself in love" (Ephesians 4:15–16).

How do we, His saints, make disciples? Primarily, we do it by participating in the building of His church. Our participation involves witnessing to our neighbors, families, and friends. It includes giving our tithe in support of our church and its mission causes. It includes giving generously to special missions offerings. It includes our participation in the Bible teaching, training classes, fellowships, ministry to shut-ins, and worship services of our church. It includes our prayer life.

By the way, as the church developed and began to appear all over the known world, Jesus' followers began to be called Christians, and their name was changed from disciples to saints. After Acts 21:16, the word *disciple* is used no more in the New Testament and the word *saint* is used fifty-seven times. A saint is one set apart. We are set apart, as specified in Ephesians 2:10, to do good works.

"Thy will be done on earth as it is in heaven." We may wonder how God's will is accomplished in heaven. We know there will be no sin in heaven, although Satan was once an angel in heaven and he rebelled and was cast out. Heaven will be different from earth in every way. The question is, Will we have free will in heaven? If we do, how is it that we will never exercise our will contrary to God's will? This is one question, along with many others, that we won't know the answer to until we get there.

The only way a lost person can do God's will is to trust Jesus for salvation. Then his life in Christ begins and one of his first responsibilities is to find God's will for his life. "Do not be conformed to this world, but be transformed by the renewing of your mind, that you may prove what the will of God is, that which is good and acceptable and perfect" (Romans 12:2).

God's will for our lives is found through prayer, Bible study, and contemplation. We must meditate on what His word and our prayers are saying to us. God opens and closes doors. He nudges us in many different ways as He guides us to do His will.

"To God be the glory for all He has done and is doing."

Notes

Our Daily Bread

"Give us this day our daily bread" (Matthew 6:11). Give us, not me, our daily bread. Again the prayer is in the plural, not the singular. Were the disciples not to pray as individuals for their daily sustenance? Were the disciples to pray as a group? I don't think this prohibits us from praying as individuals for our needs, but it does commend our participating in prayer with fellow church members and families.

How about *give*? Were the disciples encouraged to think that all they had to do was pray and God would give them their daily rations? There was a precedent for being given food. When they were in the wilderness, escaping from Egypt, God gave them manna from heaven.

In another case there were some at Thessalonica who were so sure the Lord was coming back any moment that they stopped working. This was Paul's advice to them: "For even when we were with you, we used to give you this order: if anyone will not work, neither let him eat" (2 Thessalonians 3:10).

Here is another reference to food: "Do not be anxious then, saying, 'What shall we eat?'" (Matthew 6:31). Jesus' advice to them was "But seek first His kingdom and His righteousness; and all these things shall be added unto you" (Matthew 6:33). Jesus is saying, "Get your priorities in order and all your needs will be taken care of. "Be added unto you" sounds a bit like an answer to "give us."

When Jesus was dealing with the Samaritan woman, His disciples were debating: "The disciples therefore were saying to one another, 'No one brought Him anything to eat, did he?" Jesus said to them, "My food is to do the will of Him who sent Me, and to accomplish His work" (John 4:33–34). Jesus was busy dealing with the Samaritans who had come out to see what the woman had reported to them. This was more important than eating. This is an example of keeping priorities in line. There are people who live to eat instead of eat to live.

If Jesus were here talking to us today and advising us on how to pray, I wonder if He would say the same thing. The disciples didn't have a pantry and freezer full of food and a grocery store on every corner. There are places in the world where conditions would be similar to that day, but it seems to me that we should look for a principle to guide us rather than take it literally and ask for daily bread. We certainly should continue to thank Him for our food.

The principle for me would be that we should put God first by being busy doing what we can to reach people and build His church. Food, clothing, and shelter should take a backseat and not dominate our thinking and our time.

Notes

FORGIVE OUR DEBTS

"And forgive us our debts, as we have forgiven our debtors" (Matthew 6:12). In verse 14, we are told that if we want to be forgiven for our transgressions, we must forgive those who have transgressed against us. If we want God's forgiveness, we can't continue to hold grudges against those who have harmed or offended us. This may be one of the most difficult things to understand.

What about forgiving someone who has murdered one of our loved ones? Obviously, we would have to forgive such a person. That person will be dealt with by God. Paul dealt with enemies in Romans: "Never take your own revenge, beloved, but leave room for the wrath of God, for it is written, VENGENCE IS MINE, I WILL REPAY, SAYS THE LORD" (Romans 12:19).

Refusing to forgive such a person does not mean we get even with him. Refusing to forgive him can only harm us, as we hold a grudge and continue to worry and fret. It should be satisfaction enough to know that God will handle the criminal.

Most likely, few of us will have to face such a tragic situation. Our problems are usually about dealing with much more minor infractions, such as slights, oversights, insults, gossips, thieves, debtors, disagreements, and various disagreeable situations. It is especially harmful when grudges and resentments are held among members of the church.

Another situation that is tragic is when a lost person does some harmful thing to a Christian and that Christian won't forgive the infraction. Even worse is when the Christian tries to get even and retaliates. In such cases the lost person's salvation is the most important consideration. Forgiving the guilty party could very well open up an opportunity for a witness. The overriding need in every circumstance, for the Christian, is not getting even but preserving his testimony.

One question that begs an answer is what happens to the Christian who won't forgive? We believe he cannot lose his salvation. One possibility is that he can lose the joy of his salvation. It is hard to be happy when a person is fretting over what someone has done to him. Also hanging in the balance is the need to be forgiven our transgressions. The other possibility is that the offended party is not really a Christian. He could also be a baby Christian or one who has not learned what the Bible tells him to do.

In some situations the guilty party is not even aware that he has committed the offense. It is tragic when one person is going around hurt and licking his wounds and the offending party doesn't even know about it. When the offended party offers forgiveness, it opens up the opportunity to resolve the situation.

Refusing to forgive has split churches, destroyed friendships, and harmed the witness of many Christians. I know of one person who has dropped out of church because of something done by another member. I don't know if the offending member even knows he did something. If the offended member had simply gone and talked to the person and offered forgiveness, it might well have been resolved.

Forgiving one another may be one of the greatest needs in many churches, families, and communities. We need to remember that being forgiven by God depends on our forgiving others. Unforgiven sin disrupts the fellowship we could be enjoying with our heavenly Father.

Notes

Deliver Us from Evil

"And do not lead us into temptation, but deliver us from evil. For Thine is the kingdom, and the power, and the glory, forever. Amen" (Matthew 6:13). It is interesting that the word *temptation* does not appear in the Old Testament and *tempted* appears only three times. We know that Eve was tempted by the serpent, but the word *tempted* is not used.

Who is to do the leading? The plea in the prayer is "lead us not into temptation" We know it is not God. "Let no one say when he is tempted, 'I am being tempted by God'; for God cannot be tempted by evil, and He Himself does not tempt any one" (James 1:13).

We know who does the tempting. Paul made this statement: "For this reason, when I could endure it no longer, I also sent to find out about your faith, for fear that the tempter might have tempted you, and our labor should be in vain" (1 Thessalonians 1:5). "Be of sober spirit, be on the alert. Your adversary, the devil, prowls about like a roaring lion, seeking someone to devour" (1 Peter 5:8).

We are no match for Satan if we tangle with him using our own strength. Jesus showed us how to deal with him when He was tempted in the wilderness. Jesus quoted Scripture to counter every one of the three propositions the devil made to Him.

We need at least two things to avoid yielding to temptation. First, we need to be fully committed to doing the will of God in our lives. Jesus' answers to Satan all involved His devotion to His Father. "It is written, 'MAN SHALL NOT LIVE ON BREAD ALONE, BUT ON EVERY WORD THAT PROCEEDS OUT OF THE MOUTH OF GOD" and "YOU SHALL NOT TEMPT THE LORD YOUR GOD.'" and "Be gone, Satan! For it is written, 'YOU SHALL WORSHIP THE LORD YOUR GOD, AND SERVE HIM ONLY'" (Matthew 4:4, 7, 10). Second, we need a good knowledge of the Scriptures. Bible study must be a priority in the life of the Christian.

We need to remember that we are not of this world. Man was made to have fellowship with his Creator. "for Thine is the kingdom and the power and the glory, forever." We are part of the kingdom of God. In a sense we are on a mission. Our mission is to help add people to His kingdom. Yielding to temptation and being involved with evil things prevents us from being useful in building the kingdom.

A footnote tells us that the statement "for Thine is the kingdom and the power and the glory, forever" is not included in the earliest manuscripts. It may not have been, but in the light of Scripture in other places, it is a statement of truth. When Christians yield to temptation, it destroys their witness and takes away the joy of their salvation.

It is proper for us to pray that we not be led into temptation, because the tempter is still alive and well, seeking those whom he may devour.

Notes

THE LITTLE WORD *IF*

THE WORD *IF*

Now we begin a series of devotionals on phrases in the Bible beginning with the little word *if*. The word has almost unlimited possibilities. *If* appears in the Bible about 1,570 times. *If* is a key word because it always prepares us for something to follow, such as a condition, a stipulation, or a consequence. *If* we do such and such, this is what we can expect to follow. *If* might also introduce an inquiry about what would happen *if* we did so and so.

Here are some examples: God told Moses to go to Egypt and bring out His people. Moses' response was "What *if* they will not believe me" (Exodus 4:1). This indicated a lack of faith on Moses' part. In Leviticus 4:2 we find the question, "*if* a person sins unintentionally ...," which is followed by elaborate instructions on sacrificing a bull to atone for the sin. "*If* a man makes a vow to the Lord ... he shall do according to all that proceeds out of his mouth" (Numbers 30:2). God takes our pledges and promises seriously. *If* we make a pledge, God expects us to fulfill it.

"*If* you are not careful to observe all the words of this law which are written in this book, to fear His honored and awesome name, ..." (Deuteronomy 28:58). There follows serious consequences. It took ten verses to describe all the bad things that would occur. God takes His name and His word seriously.

In Zechariah 3:7 God says, "*If* you will walk in My ways, and *if* you will perform My service, then you will also govern My house." God says *if* many times. His offers are preceded by or followed by a stipulation that requires a response on our part, and frequently the little word *if* is used. The use of *if* occurs many times in the New Testament. For example: "*If* anyone wishes to come after Me, let him deny himself, and take up his cross and follow Me" (Matthew 16:24). Jesus expects commitment from His followers. "*If* you love Me you will keep My commandments" (John 14:15).

There are some encouraging thoughts involving *ifs*. "What then shall we say to these things? *If* God is for us, who can be against us?" (Roman 8:31).

Here is one of Jesus' statements that has puzzled Christians: "Truly I say to you, if you have faith, and do not doubt, you shall not only do what was done to the fig tree, but even if you say to this mountain, 'Be taken up and cast into the sea,' it shall happen" (Matthew 21:21). For me, *mountain* doesn't mean a Mount Everest but represents difficulties and problems in life that faith in God will enable us to eliminate or overcome. We are Christ's hands, His feet, and His tongue. He depends on us to lead the lost to Himself. *If* our feet go astray and our tongues are silent, He has no other plan.

We are the Bible and the gospel for many in the world who are lost. Will they read the truth or use our example as an excuse to ignore the Savior? *If* our "script" is blurred, many will be misled and lost.

If! It is a small word with much meaning.

Notes

IF YOU PRAY

"But if any of you lacks wisdom, let him ask of God, who gives to all men generously and without reproach, and it will be given to him. But let him ask in faith without any doubting, for the one who doubts is like the surf of the sea driven and tossed by the wind. For let not that man expect that he will receive anything from the Lord" (James 1:5–7).

President Lincoln[38] said, "I have been many times to my knees by the overwhelming conviction that I had nowhere else to go."

We live in a complicated world. Who of us is wise enough to have the answers to all the questions and problems we face? We certainly lack wisdom, but God tells us in James to ask for wisdom and assures us that wisdom will then be given. Wisdom will be given if we ask in faith. We will be given it in generous amounts, *if* we do not doubt God.

Another *if:* "Again I say to you, that *if* two of you agree on earth about anything that they may ask, it shall be done for them by My Father who is in heaven. For where two or three have gathered together in My name, there I am in their midst" (Matthew 18:19–20). God honors cooperation and unity among His people, most especially in His church. This is especially true when His people gather for prayer.

A well-known and famous *if* and a much-needed prayer for our nation today is "*If* I shut up the heavens so that there is no rain, or if I command the locust to devour the land, or if I send pestilence among my people, and My people who are called by My name humble themselves and pray, and seek My face and turn from their wicked ways, then I will hear from heaven, will forgive their sin, and will heal their land" (2 Chronicles 7:13–14). It would seem that this promise was to His nation Israel, which He dealt with as a nation, but in light of other Scripture, I think the heart of this promise applies to individuals and to groups of people, especially to His church.

God doesn't play games with us. He is the ultimate loving Father. Matthew tells us, "Ask and it shall be given to you; seek and you shall find; knock and it shall be opened to you. For every one who asks receives, and he who seeks finds, and to him who knocks it shall be opened. Or what man is there among you, when his son shall ask him for a loaf, will give him a stone? Or, *if* he shall ask for a fish, he will not give him a snake, will he? *If* you then, being evil, know how to give good gifts to your children, how much more shall your Father who is in heaven give what is good to those who ask Him" (Matthew 7:7–11).

Here are some of the things that have prompted me to pray. Thoughts of a friend from the past, a near miss in heavy traffic, a beautiful sunrise or sunset, my pastor who is on vacation, a lesson I am to teach on Sunday, my lost brother, my bankrupt neighbor, the election, our president, a missionary grandson, a fellow Sunday school member scheduled for surgery, praising God for his unending supply, and on and on.

The redeemed are God's children, and He cares for His own. He hears and answers prayer!

Notes

IF YOU ABIDE IN MY WORD

This *if* is a promise: "If you abide in My word, then you are truly disciples of mine; and you shall know the truth, and the truth shall make you free" (John 8:31–21). Later John puts it a little differently: "If you abide in me, and My words abide in you, ask whatever you wish and it shall be done for you" (John 15:7).

According to *Random House Webster's College Dictionary*, "if" supposes a condition. When this condition is met, then we can expect whatever is promised to follow. If the condition is not met, then we cannot expect to receive whatever is promised.

The question is, What does it mean to abide in Jesus' word? It certainly means knowing and understanding the Word. We refer to the Bible as the Word of God, and that's what it is. It is the inspired Word of God. There are some key verses that help us understand what it means to "abide."

"Be anxious for nothing, but in everything by prayer and supplication with thanksgiving let your requests be known to God" (Philippians 4:6). This sounds like a recipe for life. Don't worry, pray about everything, and be grateful to God.

Here is a similar thought: "Rejoice always; pray without ceasing; in everything give thanks; for this is God's will for you in Christ Jesus" (1 Thessalonians 5:16–18). We may think it is difficult sometimes to know God's will, but these verses make it very clear. I wonder how often we evaluate our words and actions in light of God's Word. Probably most of us have developed a pattern of habits that we follow without asking, Is everything we do and say acceptable with God's word? I am afraid that is too true for me. How can we pray about everything?

Brother Lawrence's book *The Practice of the Presence of God* describes how we keep God in our thoughts on a continuous basis.

Frank Laubach spoke of prayer arrows. He would see someone having difficulty and just utter a prayer on that person's behalf.

When we observe a beautiful sunset or other beautiful scene, a proper response is to praise God for it.

Perhaps you have been encouraged through the years to arise early for morning devotions. That is good, but is that a good prescription for our prayer life? I wonder how we can save up all the prayer needs through the day until morning devotions. I never hear much about praying without ceasing or praying about everything. I think Scripture is telling us to be ready to pray at a moment's notice. I think this would help us avoid speaking and doing things that are less than God honoring.

Notes

If We Say, God Says

If we say, "It is impossible," God says, "The things impossible with men are possible with God" (Luke 18:27).

My eight-year-old granddaughter, Karen, talking with Bonnie, whom my son was preparing to marry, asked, "If you and Dad marry, will you have any more children?" (My son already had seven children by his first wife, who was deceased.) Bonnie answered, "We are too old to have children." Karen responded, "But with God all things are possible."

If we say, "I'm too tired," God says, "Come to Me, all who are weary and heavy-laden, and I will give you rest" (Matthew 11:28). Fear and unease are wearisome things. Jesus will relieve us of these emotions if we trust Him.

If we say, "Nobody loves me," the Bible says, "God so loved the world that he gave His only begotten Son, that whoever believes in Him should not perish but have eternal live" (John 3:16). God loves us so much that He gave His son on the cross to give us eternal life.

If we say, "I can't go on," God says, "My grace is sufficient for you, for power is perfected in weakness" (2 Corinthians 12:9). We don't have to go it alone when we have God as our heavenly Father.

If we say, "I don't know where to turn," God says, "In all your ways acknowledge Him, and He will make your paths straight" (Proverbs 3:6). Prayer gives God the opportunity to touch our minds with thoughts that show us the way in all of life.

If we say, "I am not able," God says, "God is able to make all grace abound to you, that always having all sufficiency in everything, you may have an abundance for every good deed" (2 Corinthians 9:8). When we are busy doing God's bidding, He provides for His own.

If we say, "it's not worth it," God says, "And we know that God causes all things to work together for good to those who love God, to those who are called according to His purpose" (Romans 8:28). Good from God's point of view is that which helps to shape us in the image of His son.

If we say, "I can't forgive myself," God says, "If we confess our sins, He is faithful and righteous to forgive us our sins and to cleanse us from all unrighteousness" (1 John 1:9). If God has forgiven us, what do we have to worry about?

If we say, "I can't manage," God says, "And my God shall supply all your needs according to His riches in glory in Christ Jesus" (Philippians 4:19). This promise is for those who, like the Philippians, have been generous in their support of God's work.

If we say, "I am afraid," God says, "For God has not given us a spirit of timidity, but of power and love and discipline" (2 Timothy 1:7). With God as our helper, why should we be afraid?

If we say, "I'm always worried," God says, "Casting all your anxiety upon Him, because He cares for you" (1 Peter 5:7). When we pray, we give God the opportunity to relieve our hearts of worry, because we are reminded that He does care.

I sing because I'm happy, I sing because I'm free,

For His eye is on the sparrow, and I know He watches me.

Notes

Following Jesus: Another *If*

"If any one wishes to come after me, let him deny himself, and take up his cross and follow me" (Matthew 16:24). What does it mean to come after Jesus? Is it the same as being saved, or is it an option after being saved? What does it mean to deny self? I won't pretend to answer these questions in a short devotional. We'll just nibble around the edges.

Jesus said much about what it means to love Him, to obey Him, to follow Him, to serve Him. Living a Christian life and growing as a Christian are certainly part of the answer. "Whatever you do, do your work heartily, as for the Lord rather than for men" (Colossians 3:23). This verse tells us not only to be enthusiastic about our activities and service, but to do them for the Lord and not for men. It is difficult to do things for the Lord without wondering what people think about us.

William Barclay,[39] in his commentary on Matthew says, "There is in this world all the difference in the world between existing and living. To exist is simply to have the lungs breathing and the heart beating; to live is to live in a world where everything is worthwhile, where there is peace in the soul, joy in the heart, and a thrill in every moment. Jesus gives us the recipe for life as distinct from existence."

The *Broadman Commentary*[40] explains what it means to deny self. "Denying self is not to be confused with denying something to one's self, whether it be material things, pleasure or whatever. Wicked people often deny themselves many things in order to achieve their selfish goals or conquer their enemies. Jesus meant something more radical than denying something to oneself. He meant that one must say no to oneself. A person, for the first time, becomes what he was made to be when he denies himself. One saves his life when he loses it to Christ." "Whoever wishes to save his life will lose it; but whoever loses his life for My sake shall find it" (Matthew 16:25).

Charles Sheldon, in 1896, preached some messages with the theme "What would Jesus do?" The collection became a book that sold 22 million copies. It may not always be easy to decide what Jesus would do, but we can be sure that He would always do that which is in the best interests of others.

We know, too, that today He is busy building His church. We can't go wrong when we devote our time and money to strengthening our church in its ministry and outreach to a lost and hurting world.

Think about your giving. Is it up to biblical standards? How about our time? Are we so busy with worldly things that we don't have time to serve in our church?

How often do we decide in Jesus' favor instead of what we want to do? For the sake of all whose lives we influence, let's hope we opt for Jesus.

Notes

IF I GO

Dr. Bill Bruster, our former pastor, described something I had not heard before. It pertained to the second coming of Jesus. He said, "At ancient banquets at mealtime servants would stand back until the master was finished and then they would eat. If the master was finished, he would just drop his napkin on the table. If he was leaving but intended to return, he carefully folded his napkin and laid it by his plate. This was a signal to the servant to wait."

John 20:7 tells us that when Peter entered the empty tomb, he saw the facecloth rolled up in a place by itself. The implication is that it was Jesus' way of saying, "I will be back." Jesus tells us, "And if I go and prepare a place for you, I will come again and receive you to Myself; that where I am, there you may be also" (John 14:3).

William Evans,[41] in his book *Great Doctrines of the Bible,* says, "It is claimed that one out of every thirty verses in the Bible mentions this doctrine. To every mention of His first coming the second coming is mentioned eight times." This strong emphasis in Scripture demands our attention.

We are encouraged to look for His coming: "Looking for the blessed hope and the appearing of the glory of our great God and Savior, Jesus Christ" (Titus 2:33). His coming again is an event that we are encouraged to keep looking for.

The teaching is a great comfort when we have lost a loved one or face death ourselves. "For if we believe that Jesus died and rose again, even so God will bring with Him those who have fallen asleep in Jesus ... Therefore comfort one another with these words" (1 Thessalonians 4:14, 18).

This teaching is an incentive to consistent Christian living. Most of us have asked ourselves, "Would I want to be doing this when He comes again?"

What is meant by the teaching that He is coming again? Here is how the Bible answers that question. "Men of Galilee, why do you stand looking into the sky? This Jesus, who has been taken up from you into heaven, will come in just the same way as you have watched Him go into heaven" (Acts 1:11).

"For the Lord Himself will descend from heaven with a shout, with the voice of the archangel, and with the trumpet of God; and the dead in Christ will rise first. Then we who are alive and remain shall be caught up together with them in the clouds to meet the Lord in the air, thus we shall always be with the Lord" (1 Thessalonians 4:16–17).

Finally, "Behold, He is coming with the clouds, and every eye will see Him, even those who pierced Him; and all the tribes of the earth will mourn over Him. Even so. Amen" (Revelation 1:7).

Only those who know Jesus as Savior will be happy to see His arrival. It will be a day of doom for everyone else.

Notes

IF GOD CLOTHES THE GRASS

Matthew 6:30 says, "But if God so arrays the grass of the field, which is alive today and tomorrow is thrown into the furnace, will He not much more do so for you, O men of little faith?" Contrasting us with grass, the writer reminds us that God is in charge of everything and that if He gives such good attention to temporary things, such as grass, we can expect Him to take care of our needs.

I expect many Christians, if not all of them, have enjoyed God's care and provision since they first trusted Jesus to save them. The psalmist asked, "What is man, that Thou dost take thought of him? And the son of man, that Thou dost care for him" (Psalm 8:4)? The psalmist had observed God's care and wondered why man was so special.

This short poem[42] is for those who fret and worry: Said the robin to the sparrow, "I should really like to know why these anxious human beings rush about and worry so." said the sparrow to the robin 'Friend, I think that it must be that they have no Heavenly Father such as cares for you and me."

It can be hard for older people to be optimistic and cheerful when so many parts of their bodies don't function well. But giving in to these discomforts just makes them worse. Pain and tiredness may be God's way of helping us look forward to heaven.

God's care comes with conditions and requirements. We are told not to be anxious about these necessities of life and that the Gentiles eagerly seek after these things. For us, the Gentiles refers to the unsaved. We are reminded that the heavenly Father knows that we need food, water, and clothing. Then we are told what we must do have God's provision.

"But seek first His kingdom and His righteousness; and all these things will be added to you" (Matthew 6:33). It is a matter of getting our priorities in order. If our focus is on material things, we are apt to leave God out of our life. God didn't create us to be ignored. He created us for fellowship with Himself. Once we seek God first, we have the benefit of His guidance through Scripture and prayer. We have the support of the Christian community, His church.

It is hard to explain, but it is real. Promises such as the one in Malachi 3:10 may be part of the plan. Give the tithe and God pours out blessings until there is no more need.

The cure for anxiety is not a pill or a psychiatrist but seeking first God and His righteousness.

All the people who haven't received Jesus as Savior and Lord are on their own in this complicated, cruel world. They don't have the support of the body of Christ, the church. They have to be puzzled about what happens at death. They have no hope of seeing loved ones who have gone on before.

May we be busy witnessing to the lost? Winning them to Christ will rescue them from their hopeless situation.

Notes

PROPHECIES

OF HIS COMING

The Old Testament has many references to the forthcoming Savior. So closely related are the Old Testament and New Testament references that we have to conclude we are reading the miraculous or, as we believe, divinely inspired narrative.

The prophecy: "I will surely tell of the decree of the Lord: He said to Me, 'Thou art My Son, today I have begotten thee'" (Psalm 2:7). The fulfillment: The angel said to Mary, "'You will conceive in your womb, and bear a son, and you shall name Him Jesus. He will be great, and will be called the **Son** of the Most High; and the Lord God will give Him the throne of His father David'" (Luke 1:31–32). How could the psalmist possibly have coined the words that foretold such an event? God somehow helped him. The psalmist may have been aware of the following prophecy in Genesis.

The prophecy: "And I will put enmity between you and the **woman**, And between your seed and her seed: He shall bruise you on the head, and you shall bruise him on the heel" (Genesis 3:15). The fulfillment: "But when the fullness of the time came, God sent forth His Son, born of a **woman**" (Galatians 4:4). "And Jesus, crying out with a loud voice, said 'Father, into Thy hands I commit My spirit'" (Luke 23:46). Satan had done his damage, but His access to all those who claim the crucified Savior was definitely stunted.

The prophecy: "Behold a virgin will be with child and bear a son, and she will call His name Immanuel" (Isaiah 7:14). The fulfillment: "Now the birth of Jesus Christ was as follows. When His mother Mary had been betrothed to Joseph, before they came together, she was found with child by the Holy Spirit" (Matthew 1:18). Being born of a virgin is definitely miraculous, but to tell the location of the child's birth hundreds of years beforehand magnifies the wonder of it all.

The prophecy: "But as for you, Bethlehem Ephrathah, too little to be among the clans of Judah, from you One will go forth for Me to be ruler in Israel" (Micah 5:2). The fulfillment: "Now after Jesus was born in Bethlehem of Judea in the days of Herod the King" (Matthew 2:1a).

There is even the announcement ahead of time that He was on the way.

The prophecy: "A voice is calling, clear the way for the Lord in the wilderness; Make smooth in the desert a highway for our God" (Isaiah 40:3). "Behold, I am going to send My messenger, and he will clear the way before Me" (Malachi 3:1). The fulfillment: "Now in those days John the Baptist came, preaching in the wilderness of Judea, saying, repent, for the kingdom of heaven is at hand. For this is one referred to by Isaiah the prophet, saying, The voice of one crying in the wilderness, make ready the way of the Lord" (Matthew 3:1–3).

With all the evidence that the coming of Jesus was foretold centuries before He came, it is hard to understand how anyone aware of such proof could fail to trust Him for salvation.

Actually, multitudes are unaware of these facts. It is up to us to tell them.

Notes

His Rejection, Betrayal, and Abuse

Jesus' mistreatment on the way to the cross is all prophesied. No other person can make such a claim. It is one of the realities that confirm the divine origin of the Scriptures.

The prophecy: His rejection by His brothers. "I have become estranged from my brothers and an alien to my mother's sons" (Psalm 69:8). The fulfillment: "His brothers therefore said to Him, depart from here, and go into Judea, that your disciples also may behold your works which You are doing" (John 7:3). You would think that his family, who knew about all the miraculous things related to Him, would believe He was who He claimed to be.

The prophecy: The Jewish rulers' rejection: "The stone which the builders rejected has become the chief corner stone" (Psalm 118:22). The fulfillment: "No one of the rulers or Pharisees has believed in Him, has he" (John 7:48)? Jesus was a threat to the Jewish rulers, and this blinded their eyes to Scripture that said this would happen.

The prophecy: Betrayed by a friend. "Even my close friend, in whom I trusted, who ate my bread, has lifted up his heel against me" (Psalm 41:9). The fulfillment: "I do not speak of all of you. I know the ones I have chosen; but it is that the Scripture may be fulfilled, 'He who eats My bread has lifted up his heel against Me'" (John 13:18).

The prophecy: "And I said to them, 'If it is good in your sight, give me my wages; but if not, never mind!' So they weighed out thirty shekels of silver for my wages" (Zechariah 11:12). The fulfillment: "What are you willing to give me to deliver Him up to you? And they weighed out to him thirty pieces of silver" (Matthew 26:15). Silver must not have changed in value like our money. I wonder what a dollar will be worth 2,000 years from now.

The promise: He suffered for us: "He was crushed for our iniquities; the chastening for our well-being fell upon Him, and by His scourging we are healed" (Isaiah 53:5). The fulfillment: "And they dressed Him up in purple, and after weaving a crown of thorns, they put it on Him; and they began to acclaim Him 'Hail, King of the Jews!' And they kept beating His head with a reed, and spitting at Him, and kneeling and bowing before Him" (Mark 15:17–19).

Anyone reading Isaiah 53 would have to wonder who it was talking about. The pronouns *He, Him,* and *Himself* appear forty-six times in chapter 53. The descriptions in the Old Testament and the actual experience in the New Testament are so graphically similar that it is hard to understand how anyone who knows about it could fail to believe.

Notes

HIS MINISTRY

The Old Testament prophets described Jesus' public ministry in great detail.

The prophecy: "The Spirit of the Lord God is upon Me, Because the Lord has anointed me to bring good news to the afflicted; He has sent me to bind up the broken hearted, To proclaim liberty to the captives, and freedom to the prisoners; To proclaim the favorable year of the Lord, and the day of vengeance of our God; to comfort all who mourn" (Isaiah 61:1–2). The fulfillment: "Jesus came to Nazareth, opened the book, and found the place where it was written, 'The Spirit of the Lord is upon Me, because He anointed Me to preach the gospel to the poor. He has sent Me to proclaim release to the captives, recovery of sight to the blind, to set free those who are downtrodden, to proclaim the favorable year of the Lord'" (Luke 4:17–19). Jesus went on to say in verse 21 that "Today this scripture has been fulfilled in your hearing."

What a miracle that happenings in the New Testament era were so accurately described by prophets hundreds of years earlier. This is why we read, "All Scripture is inspired by God" (2 Timothy 3:16a). There is more, much more.

The prophecy: "Galilee of the Gentiles. The people who walk in darkness will see a great light" (Isaiah 9:1b–2). The fulfillment: "And Jesus was going about in all Galilee, teaching in their synagogues and proclaiming the gospel of the kingdom, and healing every kind of disease and every kind of sickness among the people" (Matthew 4:23). That the Old Testament writers were so specific, even to the geographic references, is truly amazing.

The prophecy: "Rejoice greatly, O daughter of Zion! Shout in triumph, O daughter of Jerusalem! Behold your King is coming to you; He is just and endowed with salvation, Humble and mounted on a donkey, even a colt, the foal of a donkey" (Zechariah 9:9). The fulfillment: "Go into the village opposite you, and immediately you will find a donkey tied there and a colt with her; untie them, and bring them to Me. And when He had entered Jerusalem, all the city was stirred, saying, 'who is this?'" (Matthew 21:2, 10). This was another remarkable prophecy, fulfilled in great detail, especially the reference to the kind of transportation that Jesus would have to carry Him into Jerusalem.

The prophecy: "I will fill this house with glory, says the Lord of hosts" (Haggai 2:7b). The fulfillment: "And Jesus entered the temple and cast out all those who were buying and selling in the temple, and overturned the tables of the money changers and the seats of those who were selling doves. And He said to them, 'It is written, My house shall be a house of prayer: but you are making it a robbers den'" (Mathew 21:12–13).

Part of Jesus' ministry was setting things straight in His house of worship, the temple. When Jesus entered the temple, it was truly filled with glory, His glory as the only begotten Son of God.

Notes

His Resurrection and Reign

The prophecy: His resurrection: "For Thou wilt not abandon my soul to Sheol; neither wilt Thou allow Thy Holy One to undergo decay" (Psalm 16:10). The psalmist, centuries before Christ's crucifixion, said Christ would not stay in the grave. The fulfillment: "He is not here, for He has risen, just as He said: Come, see the place where He was lying" (Matthew 28:6). Christ not only left the tomb, but appeared to His disciples and others over a period of forty days.

Prophecy: His ascension: "Thou hast ascended on high, Thou hast led captive Thy captives" (Psalm 68:18a). The psalmist said the Savior would leave the earth. The fulfillment: "And after He had said these things, He was lifted up while they were looking on, and a cloud received Him out of their sight" (Acts 1:9). The disciples gazed into the sky while He left them. There were many witnesses to His departure.

Prophecy: His work in heaven: "He who will bear the honor and sit and rule on His throne, Thus, He will be a priest on His throne" (Zechariah 6:13). The fulfillment: "Who is the one who condemns? Christ Jesus is He who died, yes, rather who was raised, who is at the right hand of God, who also intercedes for us" (Romans 8:34).

No one can condemn those who have placed their faith in Jesus. Jesus represents us before the Father, confirming our salvation. This fulfills a promise Jesus made to His disciples while He was with them. "My sheep hear My voice, and I know them, and they follow Me; and I give eternal life to them, and they shall never perish: and no one shall snatch them out of My hand" (John 10:27–28).

Prophecy of His righteous government: "Thy throne, O God, is forever and ever; a scepter of uprightness is the scepter of Thy kingdom. Thou hast loved righteousness and hated wickedness" (Psalm 45:6–7). The fulfillment: "My judgment is just, because I do not seek my own will, but the will of Him who sent Me" (John 5:30). "In righteousness He doth judge" (Revelation 19:11).

We are concerned about those who have not heard of Jesus, and about others who are seemingly good people who don't claim Jesus and are thus condemned to hell. God is able to take care of Himself without our help. As the Bible says, His judgments are just, and those who end up in hell will know that God is just.

The prophecy: Jesus' total dominion: "May He also rule from sea to sea and from the river to the ends of the earth" (Psalm 72:8). "And to

Him was given dominion, Glory and a kingdom, that all the peoples, nations, and men of every language should serve Him" (Daniel 7:14). The fulfillment: "Therefore also God highly exalted Him, and bestowed on Him the name which is above every name, that at the name of Jesus every knee should bow, of those who are in heaven, and on earth, and under the earth, and that every tongue should confess that Jesus Christ is Lord, to the glory of God the Father" (Philippians 2:9–11).

The time will come when everyone will have to admit that Jesus is who He claimed to be. What a difference there is between confessing Jesus in this life and doing it later, when it won't save us. Pray that our witness leads some to the Savior!

Notes

THE TWENTY-THIRD PSALM

TWENTY-THIRD PSALM REVIEW

Psalm 23 is perhaps one of the best known and most loved of all the Scriptures. Its closest competitors might be the Lord's Prayer or John 3:16. This devotional is a brief look at each verse. Following this devotional will be one on each of the verses.

"The Lord is my shepherd, I shall not want" (Psalm 23:1). Sheep are dumb animals. They are totally dependent on their shepherd for sustenance and safety. The implication for us is that spiritually, we are completely dependent on God for protection from our enemy and understanding how to live this life.

"He makes me lie down in green pastures; He leads me beside still waters" (Psalm 23:2). Spiritual rest is when we have peace of mind, free from worry about our future. Sheep are afraid of water. Without God's help, there are many things to be afraid of in this life. With God's protection, we don't fear our main enemy, Satan.

"He restores my soul; He guides me in the paths of righteousness for His name's sake" (Psalm 23:3). When we trust Christ for salvation, we are made alive spiritually. As we study God's Word, He helps us know right from wrong. In this way He helps us live a life that honors Him and helps others.

"Even though I walk through the valley of the shadow of death, I fear no evil; for Thou art with me; thy rod and thy staff, they comfort me" (Psalm 23:4). As we get older, that valley gets nearer. With God's assurance, our future is with Him in heaven; we don't have to fear death. Shepherds used the staff to lift sheep out of holes they had fallen in, and to defend them against wild animals.

"Thou dost prepare a table before me in the presence of my enemies; my cup overflows" (Psalm 23:5). There is no host as gracious and generous as God. His provision is abundant. Satan must look on with jealousy when He realizes what he lost when he rebelled.

"Surely goodness and loving kindness will follow me all the days of my life, and I will dwell in the house of the Lord forever" (Psalm 23:6). God takes care of His own in this life and in the life to come. We don't deserve anything that God provides, but because He loves us, He provides for us and protects us.

It is the nature of godliness to do what is in the best interests of others. God show us the way to love. We need to emulate Him in our relationship with others.

Looking back over my life, I can see where God protected me, especially during my time in the army in World War II. He has generously provided for all of my needs and more. Even now, in old age, He has given me a wonderful wife, a great church, a large family of committed Christians, and many fine Christian friends.

"Praise God from whom all blessings flow."

Notes

HE RESTORES MY SOUL

"He makes me lie down in green pastures; He leads me beside quiet waters. He restores my soul" (Psalm 23:2–3). When we love God, His advice is in essence a command. This is the only way I can understand the phrase "He makes me." The question here is, With God having given us free will, does God *make us do anything?* One preacher said, "He provides the atmosphere that compels us to do what God wants us to do."

Whatever green pastures mean to us, to sheep it meant rest and food. The sheep were refreshed, filled, and satisfied. Green pastures for us could mean a safe, quiet place where we can feed on God's Word and be refreshed or filled.

Jesus set an example for us. After feeding the five thousand, He sent His disciples away, "and after bidding them farewell, He departed into the mountain to pray" (Mark 8:46). Here is the Lord of the universe feeling the need to get apart and pray to His father. How much more do we need to be refreshed by the Holy Spirit? Not many of us need more physical food, but most of us could benefit from more spiritual food.

"He leads me beside quiet waters." Water is one of the essentials of life. Stormy weather with torrential rain is no fun, but quiet water is refreshing. Once I was fishing with a friend in the mountains of southern Oregon, a few miles from home. We were fishing on a mountains stream that for the most part was rushing rapids. In one place I found a shaded backwater that was so still, it was like polished black marble. I lowered my hook over the water, and when it was near the surface, a foot long trout leaped from the water and grabbed the bait. I didn't think of it at the time, but looking back, that would have been an ideal place to meditate and pray.

The essence of lying down in green pastures and spending time beside quiet waters is that it restores our souls. The soul is not our spirit. In John we read, "That which is born of the flesh is flesh; and that which is born of the Spirit is spirit" (John 3:6). *Soul* could very well refer to the mind. We refer to the whole person as body, mind, and spirit. If our minds are cluttered and frustrated, we can't think straight, even about spiritual matters. Our minds definitely need to be restored on a regular basis.

In the bedlam of modern society with crowded highways, commercialism, government regulations, financial difficulties, and medical problems, many people are frustrated and uptight.

Time spent with God in a quiet place, in Bible study and prayer, is what people need to restore their peace of mind. One of my sons has a hymnbook with him during quiet time and sings to himself.

Notes

My Shepherd

"The Lord is my shepherd, I shall not want" (Psalm 23:1). This psalmist is King David. Here is a person with wealth, servants, and an army at his disposal, and yet he knew he needed God's help. He had enemies—some among his own family, even a son, and neighboring nations. If someone like David felt like a sheep needing a shepherd, how about ordinary folks like us?

Sheep are an important feature in Scripture. God chose to use them in a number of ways to show man's need and to prepare the nation of Israel for what He would do for mankind through His Son, Jesus. Sheep are mentioned 183 times in the Bible. Those who care for sheep—the shepherds—in their various forms are mentioned 110 times in Scripture.

It is interesting that God chose the shepherds in the field at night as the ones to hear the announcement of Jesus' birth.

The most interesting characteristic of sheep is their helplessness. If ever there were dumb animals, it would be sheep. Not only are they dumb, but they are defenseless. If it weren't for shepherds, animals of prey would have an easy time getting their food. These characteristics make sheep an excellent choice to represent man's need and condition.

Humans are wonderfully talented and physically strong, but spiritually they are like sheep. We were able to go to the moon, invent all kinds of helpful labor-saving devices, and fly through the air with the greatest of ease and comfort. Mentally and physically humans are very capable. Spiritually, though, we start out dead. "For all have sinned and fall short of the glory of God" (Romans 3:23). "All of us like sheep have gone astray, each of us has turned to his own way; but the Lord has caused the iniquity of us all to fall on Him" (Isaiah 53:6).

Spiritually, we need a shepherd. With the Lord as his shepherd, the psalmist said, "I shall not want." Does this mean he would never go hungry? I was wondering if this Psalm applies to the Christians in South Sudan or in other places where millions are starving. I am not smart enough to answer that question, but I have enough faith in God and the Bible to believe this Psalm applies to them as well as to us. For one thing this life is not all there is. This life is brief compared with eternity, and we will never understand everything this side of heaven.

What I do know is what Jesus told Nicodemus: "Truly, truly, I say to you, unless one is born again, he cannot see the kingdom of God" and "Truly, truly, I say to you, unless one is born of water and the Spirit, he cannot enter into the kingdom of God" (John 3:3, 5). Born of water is physical birth; born of the Spirit is to be made alive spiritually. A child of God who is faithful in prayer, study, and worship will have an understanding and a sense of God's presence in his life that, at least spiritually speaking, "he will not want."

I doubt that King David was thinking about food, clothing, and shelter when he said, "I shall not want."

Notes

He Guides Me

"He guides me in the paths of righteousness for His name's sake" (Psalm 23:3b). How does God guide? In Old Testament times, God made direct contact with Abraham, Isaac, Jacob, and Moses. For example, He talked with Moses from a burning bush and told him exactly what He wanted him to do. Moses' situation was totally different from ours. Moses had no Bible. Jesus hadn't purchased His pardon on the cross. God hadn't given Moses and the others a new heart. David declared, though, that God was guiding him. God worked through Nathan who pointed a finger at King David and declared that he was the man who had taken the lamb and killed the owner.

The Psalm wasn't written just for Old Testament times. God knew everything from the beginning to the end. He knew His son would come and die and give man the opportunity to have a new heart. He knew there would be a New Testament. He knew that the Holy Spirit would be available to convict men of their sin. However God led David in his day, our challenge is to figure out how God guides us.

Think of all the ways we have that help God enable us to know His will for our lives. We have the church with pastors and teachers. We have many Bibles and Bible-study helps. We have the story of many saints and how God led them. A few I think of are Billy Graham, Bill Wallace, Annie Armstrong, Howard Colson, and Lottie Moon. We can read their biographies and learn how God led them.

My own experience was that a few years after I was saved, I began to sense that God wanted me in work that involved more people. I thought I was going to be a mechanical engineer. My first thought was that He wanted me in education. I switched from engineering to education and taught in high school for three years.

The thought that God wanted me somewhere else never went away. Finally, after studying *Every Christian's Job,* by C. E. Matthews, I concluded that God wanted me in full-time Christian service. I decided to do that and made my decision public in my church. After that, I never had a doubt that I was where God wanted me.

I have heard others give their testimonies, and they often report having an impression that wouldn't go away until they made their decisions. I believe that God influences our minds. He lets us know when we need to make a change in our lives. He leads every Christian toward righteous living. Our Bible study, prayer life, and worship experience give God access to our minds so we can know when we are on or off the right path. It may be a guilty feeling, a sense of dissatisfaction, uneasiness, or just a sense that something is not right. The wise approach is to examine our life and try to find the cause of these feelings.

"For His name's sake." Why does God want to lead us in the paths of righteousness? Obviously, He knows it is in our best interests to live such a life. What does it have to do with His name? One thought I have is that we are His creation. What craftsman does not take pride in something he makes that is beautiful or functional? God made us, and He wants sin out of our life so He can enjoy our company.

God loves everyone and desires that all come to know Him and love Him. If His children are not living right, they will not be able to lead others to Him. "The Lord is not slow about His promise, as some count slowness, but is patient toward you, not wishing for any to perish but for all to come to repentance" (2 Peter 3:9).

It must pain God when His creation is disobedient and living lives that are harmful to themselves and to those around them, and that dishonor their Creator.

Notes

WALKING THROUGH THE VALLEY

"Even though I walk through the valley of the shadow of death, I fear no evil; for thou art with me; Thy rod and Thy staff they comfort me" (Psalm 23:4). If we live long enough, we will go through some scary valleys.

I was in the army during World War II. In the infantry my job was to be a runner. I carried messages from my outfit to other units. One night in Germany, I had to take a message through a place marked off with ribbons. The next morning, on returning, I saw why it was marked off. The area on both sides of the path was covered with shoe mines. The Germans had placed these when the ground was covered with snow, and the snow had melted, leaving the mines on the surface. They were called shoe mines because they would blow off a foot but wouldn't kill you. They would rather wound you than kill you, because wounding you tied up other soldiers who cared for you. This was not a valley, but it was dangerous place.

The psalmist is saying that when he went through scary places, he was not afraid, because he knew God would protect him. The valley of death is a scary place. We go through it when we are about to die, and we go through it when family and friends are about to die.

Death for anyone, even for Christians, is fearful. After all, we will be leaving family and friends behind. We just lost my wife's daughter to cancer. I don't think Pam was afraid of death. The night preceding her death she talked a lot and was heard saying, "Praise the Lord."

The belief that when we die, Jesus takes us to be with Himself is a great comfort. Knowing that we will see our loved ones again is a great comfort. God has given us this assurance. The Bible calls our departure sleep, not death.

The shepherd's rod and staff were used to protect the sheep. Whatever these symbolized, in the psalmist's mind, he believed God would never leave him or forsake him. We have an abundance of Scripture that gives us assurance that God will be with us through it all. The wife of Mac Moore, our minister of music at Two Rivers Baptist Church, had serious surgery. After Huntace's operation, he played the piano and sang, "Through it all, through it all, I learned to depend upon His word." It brought tears to many of us in the congregation.

For the unbeliever, facing death and danger is not only frightening but terrifying. If he has any hope of heaven, it is a false hope. God has not been his companion and friend. He doesn't know and depend on the Scriptures. All he has is his own speculation about the hereafter.

I like to think that God's Word represents His rod and staff. Whether they do or not, His word comforts me in time of trouble. May we be busy, while we have breath, helping others come to know and love our wonderful Savior?

Notes

GOD'S PROVISION AND PROTECTION

"Thou dost prepare a table before me in the presence of my enemies; Thou hast anointed my head with oil; my cup overflows" (Psalm 23:5). David recognized God as the source of his sustenance and safety.

We like to take credit for what we have. We work hard to have enough money to buy everything we need. We take out insurance to cover our house, our cars, our health, our credit, and even our future burial. We pay some company to protect our house from robbers.

Actually we would be irresponsible if we didn't do some of those things. The problem is that we get so involved in taking care of ourselves that we tend to leave God out of the picture. We may be like the ditch digger who, when asked what he was doing, said, "I digga da ditch to maka da mon to buya da bread to getta da strength to digga da ditch." Life can be like that if we leave God out.

What did David have in mind? Who were his enemies? There must have been enemies in his own household. When he sat down to eat, there may have an enemy at the table with him. One of these might have been his own son. In spite of this, David felt secure because he realized God's presence and power.

Just read what David wrote in the Psalms. Psalm 24 begins with "The earth is the Lord's, and all it contains, the world, and all those who dwell in it." The first verse of Psalm 25 is "To Thee, O Lord, I lift up my soul." Psalm 34 begins with "I will bless the Lord at all times; His praise shall continually be in my mouth."

Pogo said, "We have met the enemy and he is us." Who are our enemies? They are probably not other people. More likely they are our own selfishness, pride, laziness, stubbornness, fears, and jealousy.

We need to be more like David. He was very conscious of God's power and presence in his life. He spent time in prayer. Jesus put it this way: "Do not be anxious then, saying, 'What shall we eat?' or 'What shall we drink?' or 'With what shall we clothe ourselves?' For all these things the Gentiles eagerly seek; for your heavenly Father knows that you need all these things. But seek first His kingdom and His righteousness; and all these things will be added to you" (Matthew 6:31–33).

As for the future, Jesus went on to say, "Therefore do not be anxious for tomorrow, for tomorrow will care for itself. Each day has enough trouble of its own" (Matthew 6:34).

It's not that we shouldn't have concern for our safety and the necessities of life. It is a matter of priorities and faith. After all, Paul said, "If anyone will not work, neither let him eat" (2 Thessalonians 3:10b).

Our most important need is learning how to put God first. These verses in First Thessalonians say it best: "Rejoice always; pray without ceasing; in everything give thanks; for this is God's will for you in Christ Jesus" (1 Thessalonians 5:16–18).

Notes

Goodness and Loving Kindness

"Surely goodness and loving kindness will follow me all the days of my life, and I will dwell in the house of the Lord forever" (Psalm 23:6). Instead of *surely* another reference gives *only* as a possibility. *Only* sounds more certain that *surely*. Whichever it is, David believed that God would take care of him.

Goodness and kindness are listed in the fruit of the Spirit. Love is another fruit. Perhaps *loving kindness* meant that the kindness that was in David's best interests was the kindness that he would experience. It is possible that some experiences that are good for us don't seem to be so kind at the time. We can wonder if David considered hiding in a cave, to escape King Saul's executioners, would fit in the category of goodness and loving kindness.

Romans 8:28 comes to mind. We know that David loved God, and he certainly felt called by God to be king. The circumstances of his being chosen and crowned by Samuel would have convinced him that he was chosen by God to succeed King Saul. Did everything work together for good in David's life? I suppose there are some questions for which we'll have to wait for answers until we're in heaven.

More important for us is to consider whether we can say the same thing. Have goodness and loving kindness followed us all the days of our lives? I for one have no complaints. God has been good to me. Jean and I have more than thirty grandchildren and great-grandchildren. All of them who are of age are saved.

We have good health for our age and are able to be engaged in the Lord's service through our church. We have many good friends. We can say that goodness and loving kindness have followed us thus far. We have both lost loved ones, but we have confidence that they are with the Lord, and that is a great comfort.

David said, "I will dwell in the house of the Lord forever." We don't know what David's concept of heaven was. Some of the references to heaven refer to the sky above the Earth. All totaled there are about 315 references to heaven and the heavens in the Old Testament and 361 in the New. The house of the Lord could refer to the temple, but David could not have thought he would dwell in the temple and live there forever.

We have it much better and clearer than David. He looked forward to a savior, but we live after the fact. Jesus has come, was crucified, buried, resurrected, and ascended into heaven. We have the whole account in the New Testament. Jesus has said He will come and receive us unto Himself and we will be with Him forever.

The Twenty-third Psalm is beautiful. David was a man and had his flaws like every other human. He loved the Lord, and we are the beneficiaries of his poetic genius.

Notes

LOVE

FAITH

"But now abide faith, hope, love, these three; but the greatest of these is love" (1 Corinthians 13:13). To explain faith with a few words is like trying to float a cruise liner in a bathtub. "Now faith is the assurance of things hoped for, the conviction of things not seen" (Hebrews 11:1). Words used in other translations are *assurance of, confident assurance of, solid ground of, being sure, the title deed, substance to,* and *the realization of.*

It doesn't take faith to believe in the things we can see. Faith involves confidence in God, assurance that He will do what He has promised in Scripture. "Behold, as for the proud one, His soul is not right within him; but the righteous will live by his faith" (Habakkuk 2:4). This is the reference made in Romans 1:17: "The righteousness of God is revealed from faith to faith: as it is written, But the righteous man will live by faith."

These verses are what drove Martin Luther out of the Catholic Church. In the Bible *believe* appears at least 292 times, *faith* 380 times, and *trust* 138 times. These three words are used for a total of at least 810 times. In *Dictionary of the Bible*[43] there is a small paragraph of discussion about the word *believe.* The entry for trust says "see faith." There are two large pages of fine print that refer to *faith.*

Grammatically speaking, *faith* is a noun and *believe* is a verb. Our faith is what we have, and believe is what we do. Our faith is what enables us to believe. It is the basis for believing. "He who believes in the Son has eternal life" (John 3:36). Faith is what enables us to act on what we understand God to be telling us in the Bible.

The more we study the Scripture, understand its meaning, and then act on it, the stronger our faith becomes. Living a life of faith, as God again and again does what He says in the Bible He will do, develops our confidence as Christians much the same way that doing calisthenics strengthens us physically. Experiences in life that demonstrate the reality of God also strengthen our faith.

One day on the way home from work, I suddenly decided to stop for peaches at a roadside market. I made a quick lane change and in the process cut a little too close to a car behind me. As I pulled off the road for the peaches, this car also pulled off a few yards in front of me. The driver proceeded to open his trunk, get out a tire iron, and head toward me. Before he could get to me, four or five men surrounded me. I don't know where they came from except that one or two of them had to cross a busy highway to get to me. When the offended man saw the men around me, he stopped and went back to his car.

Did God alert these men to my dilemma? I don't know how they could have sensed the situation so quickly if He had not.

That experience certainly strengthened my faith.

Notes

HOPE

Some words that relate to the concept of hope are *comfort, expectation, confidence, trust, endurance,* and *patience.* Hope is one of the three great graces found in 1 Corinthians 13:13: faith, hope, and love.

"All have sinned and fall short of the Glory of God" (Romans 3:23, HCSB). But "God wanted to make known among the Gentiles the glorious wealth of this mystery, which is Christ in you, the hope of glory" (Colossians 1:27, HCSB). Whatever God's glory is, we lose it because of sin. Our hope of regaining it is Christ in us through our faith.

"Therefore, since we have been declared righteous by faith, we have peace with God through our Lord Jesus Christ. We have also obtained access through Him by faith into this grace in which we stand, and we also rejoice in the hope of the glory of God. And not only that, but we also rejoice in our afflictions, because we know that affliction produces endurance, endurance produces proven character, and proven character produces hope" (Romans 5:1–5, HCSB).

With Christ in us, even the tough circumstances in life do not destroy our hope. When we have come through critical times with Christ's help, the experience makes us stronger.

"Now in this hope we were saved, yet hope that is seen is not hope because who hopes for what he sees?" (Romans 8:24, HCSB). "Rejoice in hope; be patient in affliction; be persistent in prayer" (Romans 12:12, HCSB). We can rejoice even when in pain, but it is not automatic without our involvement. It requires our patience and persistence in prayer.

"This hope we have as an anchor for our lives, safe and secure" (Hebrews 6:19, HCSB). This is a hope that serves as an anchor to keep us from drifting away from God's will for our lives.

"Put on a helmet of the hope of salvation" (1 Thessalonians 5:8b, HCSB). Hope is our protective helmet. The head is where our mind is. It is our mind that the "hope of salvation" protects when we are confronted with false religions and cults. The assurance of our salvation in Christ keeps us from being taken in by error.

"He poured out this Spirit on us abundantly through Jesus Christ our Savior, so that having been justified by His grace, we may become heirs with the hope of eternal life" (Titus 3:6–7, HCSB). Our hope for a future life is in Christ Jesus our Lord.

Our hope is supported by Christ's resurrection and ascension and is assured by the indwelling Holy Spirit. Hope enables us to endure the hardships of this life with joy in our hearts. Hope enables those who are persecuted to face the enemy with courage.

Knowing our future is in heaven, with Christ for all eternity, makes the pain and hurt in this life easier to bear.

Notes

Love

The third of the three great graces is love. There are lots of ways to think about love: our love for family, friends, associates for God the Father and Jesus; God's love for man and for Jesus; and Jesus' love for the Father. The subject would fill several books. In a sense the Bible is God's love letter to man.

The Bible uses two words to discuss the concept of love: *phileo,* which speaks of brotherly love and *Agape,* which is God-like love. Phileo is used 12 times in the Old Testament and 22 times in the New Testament. Agape, in its various forms, appears 268 times in the Old Testament and 254 times in the New Testament. Agape is God-like love. It is what we do. The Bible gives much more attention to agape love than phileo love. Agape love means that we do for others what is in their best interests.

Here are some of the more familiar Bible verses on the subject. "By this all men will know that you are My disciples, if you have love for one another" (John 13:35). We can't pick and choose who to love and who not to. It doesn't mean we have to associate with everyone, but when we do have contact with them, we are obligated to do that which is in their best interests.

"If I speak with the tongues of men and of angels, but do not have love, I have become a noisy gong or a clanging cymbal" (1 Corinthians 13:1). Noisy gongs and clanging symbols are very annoying. "Above all, keep fervent in your love for one another, because love covers a multitude of sins" (1 Peter 4:8). The "one another" in this verse certainly includes fellow church members. This would include the pastor, and it would not be in his best interests for us to criticize him.

"You shall love the Lord your God with all your heart, and with all your soul, and with all your strength, and with all your mind; and your neighbor as yourself" (Luke 10:27). In the parable of the Good Samaritan, Jesus identified a neighbor as a person in need. *With heart, soul, strength, and mind* means that we must love that neighbor with our entire being. If we are to love any person in need, even our enemies, how much more are we to love our family members, immediate neighbors, and fellow church members?

We must love them and do what is in their best interest, even if we don't like them. We can never go wrong by doing too much, but we can go wrong by doing nothing.

It is not always easy to know what to do. An experience I had, when teaching school, involved some twin brothers. I had befriended them. I had gone out of my way to help them. Then one day one of them did something I couldn't overlook, and I had to reprimand him for it. That one experience erased all the good things I had done for them. After that, neither of them would speak to me without a frown. I had to wonder if I had done the right thing.

The love the Bible speaks of is an act of the will, not of emotion. Again, we don't have to like everyone, but we do have to love them.

Notes

A *Love* Acrostic

"**Let** love be without hypocrisy" (Romans 12:9). Our love for each other must be genuine, not artificial. There are situations where a person is overly friendly because he wants something. I got a call from someone asking for money for a worthy cause. He started out using my first name and calling me buddy. He was a stranger. How could his familiarity be genuine?

There are people who habitually speak in an overly friendly manner to everyone one in every situation. Such behavior doesn't seem genuine. It would seem to me that the way we relate to each other requires a degree of thought so that what we say or what we do is appropriate to the needs of the other person.

Love **One** another. "Fervently love one another from the heart" (1 Peter 1:22b). This seems to say we should be enthusiastic in the way we relate to each other. Personality has a lot to do with how we act. Some of us are introverts and others are extroverts. It requires more effort for us introverts to be enthusiastic in our relationship with others.

We can't let our personality cause people to think we are unfriendly or uninterested in them. Enthusiasm can be cultivated. We just have to try a little harder than the extroverts. In 1 John chapters 3 and 4 we find the word *love* thirty times. References to brothers and to one another occur fifteen times. John even indicates that how we relate to each other is evidence of whether we have been born again or not.

"**Very** highly in love." I found this passage: "But we request of you, brethren, that you appreciate those who diligently labor among you, and have charge over you in the Lord and give you instruction, and that you esteem them **very** highly in love because of their work" (1 Thessalonians 5:12–13). Teachers and other leaders are held to a higher standard because they can do so much damage if they go wrong. Sometimes they are under great pressure because of their responsibilities. Our encouragement can mean a whole lot to them. Encouraging them and complimenting them is one way we can love them.

I have always commended my pastors for their sermons. We can find something good in every sermon. If we were in the pastor's shoes, we would discover how difficult it is to decide what to preach. How do you always have something pertinent for everyone in the congregation? There are all age groups and new and mature Christians. There are people with all levels of education in most congregations.

So much rides on the work of our pastors, who are human like the rest of us. Even if for some reason we don't like our pastor, we are told in this verse to encourage them for the sake of their work. Our encouragement is in their best interests and as such is an expression of agape love.

Each other. "And be kind to one another, tender hearted, forgiving **each** other, just as God in Christ Jesus also has forgiven you" (Ephesians 4:32). "Bearing with one another, and forgiving **each** other, whoever has a complaint against anyone; just as the Lord forgave you, so also should you" (Colossians 3:13). Forgiving each other for whatever slight or harm a person is guilty of is a very clear command in the Scriptures.

It may be that there are people who used to be in a Sunday school class or other group who are now missing. It could be that, even without knowing it, someone said something, did something, or failed to do something to which the missing person took offense. We need to be careful in our conversations and actions so that we encourage and do not discourage **each** other.

Maintaining warm, friendly relationships among the members of a church is vital to the success of that church's outreach and ministry efforts. It is the way those outside the church are led to say, "See how they love one another."

Notes

God's Love for Us

God loves us and cares for us even though there are times when we have doubts. "And we know that God causes all things to work together for good to those who love God, to those who are called according to His purpose. For whom He foreknew, He also predestined to become conformed to the image of His son, That He might be the first-born among many brethren" (Romans 8:28–29). What is good from God's perspective is different from ours. Anything that causes us to become more like Jesus is good from God's point of view, even though sometimes the experience is painful.

"Cast your burden on the Lord and He will sustain you; He will never allow the righteous to be shaken" (Psalm 55:22). "Casting all your anxiety upon Him, because He cares for you" (1 Peter 5:7). "Come to me all who are weary and heavy-laden, and I will give you rest" (Matthew 11:28).

Jesus cares for and comforts us in all our difficult times. His care is so complete that He doesn't even want us to be anxious. By depending on God, we can avoid a life of tension and worry.

God is a great leader. He delegates responsibility. He expects us to help in caring for people. "Bear one another's burdens and thus fulfill the law of Christ" (Galatians 6:2). One church's plan puts each Sunday school class on a team with the deacons. Sunday school leaders and members in that plan are charged with helping to care for members and prospects. This is something they may have always done, but now with greater emphasis and organization.

I heard Dr. James Sullivan, former president of the Baptist Sunday School Board (now LifeWay Christian Resources), define *organization* as the "equitable distribution of a workload and the synchronization of a work effort." There is much work to be done by our churches, and it is shameful when we don't do in a properly organized way.

Easter reminds us just how much God loves us. Dying in our place He took care of our greatest need—our sin problem. Read John 3:16 and substitute *me* for *world*. "For God so loved *me,* that He gave his only begotten Son, that if *I* believe in Him I would not perish, but have eternal life."

Here is one of my favorite choruses: "Are there any rivers that seem to be uncross-able, are there any mountains you cannot tunnel through? God specializes in things that seem impossible. He knows a thousand ways to make a way for you. Let go and let God have His wonderful way. Let go and let God have His way. Your troubles will vanish, your night turn to day. Let go and let God have his way."

God's way for us is the only way to true happiness. His love for us is real. As our heavenly Father, He cares for us, provides for us, protects us, and saves us for an eternity with Him in heaven.

Notes

OTHERS

A PLACE FOR YOU

"Let not your heart be troubled; believe in God, believe also in Me. In My father's house are many dwelling places; if it were not so, I would have told you; for I go to prepare a place for you. And if I go and prepare **a place for you**, I will come again, and receive you to Myself; that where I am there you may be also" (John 14:1–3). This is one of the most precious promises in the entire Bible. With heaven as our final destination, there is no reason for our hearts to be troubled.

Jesus challenged us to believe in God and in Himself. It is good for a person to ask himself, Do I really believe in God and in His Son Jesus? Later in verse 15 in this chapter of John, Jesus explained how we can know if we believe in Him. He said, "If you love Me you will keep My commandments." In another place, when Jesus was asked which was the greatest commandment, His answer was "You shall love the Lord your God with all your heart, and with all your soul, and with all you mind. This is the great and foremost commandment. And the second is like it, you shall love your neighbor as yourself" (Matthew (22:37–39).

One way to know if we love God is ask ourselves if we love our neighbor. Not the friendly good-looking neighbor but all our neighbors. The kind of love we are to have is agape love. This means we do that which is in the best interest of our neighbor. *Neighbor* isn't limited to the people who live next door to us.

We know that Jesus has gone. Luke records this at the end of his gospel and in Acts 1:9: "And after he had said these things, He was lifted up while they were looking on, and a cloud received Him out of their sight." In verse 11 two men in white clothing said, "This Jesus, who has been taken up from you into heaven, will come in just the same way as you have watched Him go into heaven."

What about this place where Jesus has gone? The word *heaven* appears in the Bible nearly 450 times—about 225 times in each of the Old and New Testaments. Most of the description of heaven is in the last two chapters of Revelation. We are told in 21:4: "He shall wipe away every tear from their eyes; and there shall no longer be any death; there shall no longer be any mourning or crying or pain." Verse 20 tells us that the streets of heaven are pure gold. The thing that people think is so precious here will be pavement in heaven. We won't just sing and praise the Lord all the time, because verse 5 in chapter 22 says that "they shall reign forever and forever." We will be responsible for overseeing something. Daniel 7:18 says, "But the saints of the Highest One will receive the kingdom and possess the kingdom forever, for all ages to come."

This life is like a vapor or like the grass of the fields—here today and gone tomorrow when compared with eternity. What a blessing it is to know that our future is in the hands of the One who made the heavens and the earth.

Notes

AVOIDING CONFLICTS

Paul wrote to some friends in Philippi, saying, "I urge Euodia and I urge Syntyche to live in harmony in the Lord" (Philippians 4:2). Then he appealed to one of his comrades to help these women, who had worked with him in the cause of the gospel. We don't know the nature of the conflict between these two women, but apparently it was interfering with their ministry. Just in passing it is interesting to note that there is just one consonant in Euodia and only one vowel in Syntyche. Their names couldn't be any more different.

Sometimes it is the difference in personalities that causes conflict. One person is eager to get things done and another is sort of laid-back. There is a time and place for which each of these personalities is an advantage, but when they are working on the same project, there can be conflict.

In church life people differ in the type of music they prefer or the style of preaching they like. This happens because God made us different. Wouldn't it be boring if we were carbon copies of each other? Differences make life interesting but at the same time can be the source of conflict.

Paul challenged the Philippians in chapter 2, verse 2 "To make his joy complete by being of the same mind, maintaining the same love, united in spirit, intent on one purpose." Having one purpose, such as reaching the lost for Christ, should motivate us to overcome our differences. Our relationships can be enhanced in many ways. We can think of ways to encourage each other. Everyone needs to be affirmed.

We can get better acquainted with each other. When people step on our toes, rub us the wrong way, or hurt our feelings, we don't have to blow a fuse. After all, Jesus did tell us to turn our other cheek. We can assume they didn't know they offended us, and most of the time that would be true.

On the other hand what they said could be true; perhaps they pointed to one of our faults. It would be our pride that caused us to be offended. It takes courage to say thank you and then to go on and correct the thing that the friend highlighted.

Later in chapter 2 Paul said in verse 14, "Do all things without grumbling or disputing." Our love for one another compels us to give the benefit of the doubt, turn the other cheek, forgive each other, and pray for each other. This expectation of us may be one of the reasons Paul said in verse 23, "I can do all things through Him who strengthens me."

There will always be conflicts, disagreements, hurt feelings, toes stepped on, slights, and feeling rubbed the wrong way, but how we handle these things is one of the ways Christians are different from the rest of the world. The way we get along is part of our testimony before those who don't know Jesus.

It is a tragedy when Christians squabble, and lost people and young Christians are turned away from Christ and the church. What a difference it makes when they can see us and say, "They really love each other."

Notes

Being Salt and Light

Jesus very clearly tells us what He wants us to be in this life. In Matthew 5:13–14 Jesus tells us that we are to be the salt of the earth and the light of the world. We've heard this taught and preached, but how hard have we tried to be salt and light?

Salt does several worthwhile things. It flavors and preserves our food, it helps us make homemade ice cream, and it melts ice so we don't slip on the sidewalk going after the morning paper in the wintertime.

How does a Christian be salt? Salt adds flavor to food. We don't need to be the life of the party, but we can be positive and cooperative. When there is work to be done, we can pitch in and help, and perhaps others will join us. I have noticed when out camping with a group that some will gather wood and do other things to get ready while some are content to just sit and talk.

Christians have an opportunity in a worrisome world to demonstrate what Christ does to help a person remain calm and contented. When others are worried and fretting, the Christian who is calm and satisfied tends to moderate any situation, and that helps to preserve everyone's sanity. One function of salt is to preserve or prevent spoilage. Many churches have split over differences of opinion about minor things. A church is fortunate if some member has the ability to moderate the situation and thus preserve the church. That person would be salt.

Christians are also to be the light of the world. Jesus is the light of the world. Our part is to reflect His light. We do that when Jesus takes up residence in our heart so that His attitude toward people and situations becomes our attitude toward people and life around us.

"I have been crucified with Christ; and it is no longer I who live, but Christ who lives in me; and the life which I now live in the flesh I live by faith in the Son of God, who loved me and delivered Himself up for me" (Galatians 2:20). Matthew 5:16 continues by saying, "That they may see your good works and glorify your Father who is in heaven." Christians help society solve problems by bringing the light of Scripture to bear on situations.

There is a little poem titled "Don't Be What You Isn't." We need to know what we are. How could we have a greater authority than the One who made us in the first place? If our Lord Jesus says we are salt and light, then that is what we are.

We cannot be salt and light if we haven't met the Savior. It is the presence of the Holy Spirit in our hearts that changes our personality and helps us be what God wants us to be—salt and light.

Notes

FELLOWSHIP—ONE ANOTHER

"If we walk in the light as He Himself is in the light, we have fellowship with one another, and the blood of Jesus His Son cleanses us from all sin" (1 John 1:7). We have fellowship with one another, but I wonder if it is the type of fellowship that is described in Scripture. We greet each other with a hug or a handshake and talk about the weather and the latest ball game. We eat together and brag or complain about the meal. We even sit together in worship services and afterward share comments about the music and the sermon, even though we may have slept through part of it. Sometimes we compliment the service and other times we complain about it.

I think John is talking about a different kind of fellowship. It starts out with the condition that we are "walking in the light as He is in the light." What would walking in the light, as He does, have to do as a condition for fellowship? It could mean that we are honest with each other. It could mean that we have real concern for the welfare of each other.

Later John says, "If we confess our sins, He is faithful and righteous to forgive our sins and to cleanse us from all unrighteousness" (John 1:9). Why is John talking about sin and forgiveness and fellowship with one another all in the same breath? It must mean that in Bible study and worship together, we are able to share our inmost thoughts and in the light of God's Word help each other recognize sin in our lives.

James says, "Therefore, confess your sins to one another, and pray for one another so that you may be healed" (James 5:16). I have often wondered if I have been sensitive enough about sin in my life to always be specific when asking for forgiveness. Our prayers often include the general request to God to "forgive our sins."

The kind of fellowship Scripture speaks of could mean we trust each other enough to talk about our tempers, our critical spirits, our pride and selfishness, and the way we worry and fret. We are usually ready to share our accomplishments and successes and other positive things in our life, but we have to be careful that this doesn't involve the sin of pride and boasting.

How fortunate we are when we have the kind of friends with whom we can be open and aboveboard, the kind with whom we can share and whose advice we can seek on personal matters.

Even though many Christians have fellowship with friends at church, in their classes, ministries, and socials, there is reason to wonder if it has the depth and meaning of the biblical "fellowship with one another."

Notes

Forgetting and Remembering

A word study turns up some interesting questions. All forms of the word *forget* turn up 111 times in the Old Testament and only 9 times in the New Testament. All forms of the word *remember* show up 206 times in the Old Testament and 48 times in the New Testament. It seems that remembering is more important in the Bible—especially in the New Testament—than forgetting. This study was in the New American Standard Exhaustive Concordance of the Bible. The count would probably vary some in other translations.

One of the most familiar uses of *forgetting* is Paul's: "Brethren, I do not regard myself as having laid hold of it yet; but one thing I do: forgetting what lies behind and reaching forward to what lies ahead, I press on toward the goal for the prize of the upward call of God in Christ Jesus" (Philippians 33:13–14).

God is busy shaping His children in the image of Christ. We like Paul should not let past failures and experiences get in God's way of shaping us. Worrying about what might have been or fretting about some failure or misstep is better forgotten. Glowing in some past achievement or holding grudges that cripple our spirit should be buried. Better to forgive and forget and do as Paul did—forget the past and focus on what Jesus wants of us in worship, witness, and ministry.

Then it is encouraging to remember God's promises. In Isaiah 43:25 God says, "I, even I, am the one who wipes out your transgressions for my own sake; and I will not remember your sins." It is good for us to remember what it felt like when we first accepted Jesus as our Lord and Savior. What a relief it was to know that God forgave us and made us His children.

When we participate in the Lord's Supper, we are told in 1 Corinthians 11:24–25 to remember His body and His blood that were sacrificed for our salvation. "He made Him who knew no sin to be sin on our behalf, that we might become the righteousness of God in Him" (1 Corinthians 5:21). He has given us Christ's righteousness, which is what He sees when He looks at us.

The Scripture advises us to not be forgetful hearers. I know I hear a lot of things that I can't recall an hour later. How many of us can remember last Sunday's sermon topic? James speaks to this: "But one who looks intently at the perfect law, the law of liberty, and abides by it, not having become a forgetful hearer but an effectual doer, this man shall be blessed in what he does" (James 1:25).

We hear much from the Bible every week in Sunday school and worship services. Our responsibility is to listen carefully and make the adjustments in life that the Lord lays on our hearts as we listen to His word being preached and taught.

Notes

Blessed Assurance

The Lord is my Shepherd, I shall not want. Jesus loves me, this I know. For the Bible tells me so. Blessed assurance, Jesus is mine. "But you are a chosen race, a Royal Priesthood, A Holy Nation, A PEOPLE FOR God's OWN POSSESSION, that you may proclaim the excellences of Him who has called you out of darkness into His marvelous light" (1 Peter 2:9). What a blessing it is to know that we have been saved and are no longer spiritually blind.

"For God so loved the world, that He gave His only begotten Son, that whoever believes in Him should not perish, but have eternal life" (John 3:16). "Therefore if any man is in Christ, he is a new creature; the old things passed away; behold, new things have come" (2 Corinthians 5:17). In Christ we are brand new. "He made Him who knew no sin to be sin on our behalf, that we might become the righteous of God in Him" (2 Corinthians 5:21). This verse tells us that the gift God has given us is the sinless perfection of Christ. When God looks at us after we are saved, He doesn't see our sin but sees the righteousness of Jesus.

"And we know that God causes all things to work together for good to those who love God, to those who are called according to His purpose. For whom He foreknew, He also predestined to become conformed to the image of His Son, that He might be the first born among many brethren" (Romans 8:28–29). God is busy working with everything to make us more like Jesus. "It is God who is at work in you, both to will and to work for His good pleasure" (Philippians 2:13). We are not to just lie back and let God work on us. He expects our cooperation.

To the Philippians, who had been more generous than other churches in their support of him, Paul gave them this assurance in chapter 4, verse 19: "And my God shall supply all your needs according to His riches in glory in Christ Jesus." This sounds familiar: "'Bring the whole tithe into the storehouse, so that there may be food in My house, and test Me now in this,' says the Lord of hosts, 'if I will not open for you the windows of heaven, and pour out for you a blessing until there is no more need'" (Malachi 3:10). God does love a cheerful giver. May we always be generous in support of our church, and through our church, and support our missions through the several offerings. God will love our cheerful generosity, and He will take care of us.

We are truly blessed with the assurance that we are under God's care now and for all eternity. That is the precious possession of those who placed their faith in the Lord Jesus Christ and strive to do His will in this life.

Notes

CHRISTIAN FELLOWSHIP

"If we walk in the light as He Himself is in the light, we have fellowship with one another, and the blood of Jesus His Son cleanses us from all sin" (1 John 1:7). Christians enjoy talking and singing together as Ephesians 5:19 recommends: "speaking to one another in psalms and hymns and spiritual songs, singing and making melody with your heart to the Lord." One of our church's best services is the Classic Service on Sunday evening. We enjoy singing the old hymns. One of the best fellowship times are the rehearsals and singing events with the senior adult choir, the Good Life Singers.

The morning services in our church have some of the best music with the choir, special groups, solos, and congregational singing. "Let the word of Christ richly dwell within you, with all wisdom teaching and admonishing one another with psalms and hymns and spiritual songs, singing with thankfulness in your hearts to God" (Colossians 3:16). When we pay attention to the words in the hymns, we learn a lot by singing together.

We study together in our Sunday school classes. I haven't noticed much "admonishing one another." Perhaps we should challenge each other more than we do. Many of our members don't attend Sunday school. The early Christians set a great example for us. In Acts 2:42 we are told that "they were continually devoting themselves to the apostles' teaching and to fellowship, to the breaking of bread and to prayer." One element of Christian fellowship is just being together, studying, singing, praying, talking, and eating.

One of the most important parts of fellowship is ministering to one another. There is this admonition: "Bear one another's burdens, and thus fulfill the law of Christ. So then, while we have opportunity, let us do good unto all men, especially to those who are of the household of faith" (Galatians 6:2, 10). We are to give special attention to our brothers and sisters in Christ.

We are supposed to motivate each other to do the things God intended us to do when He saved us. "And let us consider how to stimulate one another to love and good deeds" (Hebrews 10:24). I think most of us need a little gentle push once in a while. Scripture condones that thought. "Not forsaking our own assembling together, as is the habit of some, but encouraging one another; and all the more, as you see the day drawing near" (Hebrews 10:25).

When it comes to assembling together, we shouldn't make decisions about attending our church's services on the basis of who the preacher is or what special attraction is scheduled. There will always be opportunities to encourage some of our fellow believers, even if we aren't excited about the agenda.

Our consideration of fellowship has used many words such as *talking, singing, admonishing, challenging, teaching, ministering, stimulating, encouraging,* and *eating together.* The concept has an important place in Scripture and thus must have an important place in our lives.

Notes

FAITH VERSUS FEAR

The Bible uses both *faith* and *fear* an almost equal number of times. *Faith* appears 240 times in the New Testament compared with only 4 times in the Old Testament. *Fear* appears 225 times in the Old Testament compared with 74 times in the New. Although *faith* is used only a few times in the Old Testament, *belief* and *believe* are used 37 times but more than 300 times in the New Testament. It must be significant that *fear* is used more than three times as much in the Old Testament as in the New, whereas *faith* and *belief* are used 18 times as often in the New Testament.

We know that in the Old Testament dispensation, people lived under law. It is easy to understand how they could be fearful that they had broken a law; atoning for their sin meant killing sheep and sprinkling blood. There are references in Hebrews that say Abel, Enoch, Abraham, and Noah had faith, but the Old Testament accounts that are referenced do not use the word *faith*. Their actions demonstrated their belief in God.

We use *faith* and *belief* interchangeably. *Fear* sometimes means "awe" or "to show reverence," and other times it means "to be afraid." "But for you who fear My name the son of righteousness will rise with healing in its wings; and you will go forth and skip about like calves from the stall" (Malachi 4:2). That use of *fear* means "awe" or "reverence." Philippians 1:14b says, "Most of the brethren ... speak the word of God without fear," meaning they were without cause to be afraid. The main use of the word *faith* is in reference to our relationship to Jesus.

A passage in Galatians contains one of the most beautiful explanations of the place of faith in our life: "But before faith came, we were kept in custody under the law, being shut up to the faith which was later to be revealed. Therefore the Law has become our tutor to lead us to Christ, that we may be justified by faith. But now that faith has come, we are no longer under a tutor. For you are all sons of God through faith in Christ Jesus" (Galatians 3:23–26).

A poem titled "Faith Casts Out Fear" sounds like a verse of Scripture, but I looked and couldn't find one. What I did find was this verse: "There is no fear in love; but perfect love casts out fear, because fear involves punishment, and the one who fears is not perfected in love" (1 John 4:18).

The word *perfect,* as used here, does not mean "flawless" but "mature." None of us is perfect, in the sense of having no flaws, but we can have a mature faith. Our faith in Christ enables us to love and that love gets rid of our fear. We no longer fear God's judgment. We need not fear the future because of our faith in Jesus.

Spending time is Bible study, prayer, and fellowship with other believers helps us face life without fear.

Faith in Jesus Removes Fear

Pay attention to Jesus, who rescued you from sin.
When difficulty assails and fears surround,
Look to Jesus and His word.
He will remove your fear and give you hope.

Notes

GOOD GRIEF

Our church had three funerals last week. We went to the one for a retired preacher. His funeral, like ones we have been to for many Christians, was more a celebration of his life than a weeping for his passing. I have been to funerals for unsaved people, and the contrast is remarkable. Instead of rejoicing over a life well lived, there was weeping and wailing. Why the difference? For one thing the passing of a saint is not seen as death but as a passing from this life to life in heaven with the Lord.

Jesus said to the thief next to Him on the cross, "I assure you: Today you will be with me in Paradise" (Luke 23:43, HCSB). He didn't say tomorrow or next year or someday but "today." If a thief who believed in Jesus for only hours before he died went on to be with Jesus in paradise that day, there is no reason for any Christian to fear death.

Our Lord doesn't want us to grieve like those who don't know Him. "We do not want you to be uninformed, brothers, concerning those who are asleep, so that you will not grieve like the rest, who have no hope" (1 Thessalonians 4:13, HCSB). We are not to grieve like those who have not received Jesus as their savior.

When Jesus knew that Lazarus had died, He said to the disciples, "Our friend Lazarus has fallen asleep, but I'm on My way to wake him up" (John 11:11b, HCSB). Later Jesus said to Martha, "I am the resurrection and the life. The one who believes in Me, even if he dies, will live. Everyone who lives and believes in Me will never die" (John 11:25–26, HCSB).

Death for us is so disruptive. When Carol, my first wife, died, I got a letter from my niece in which she said, "It leaves a big hole." That explained the experience for me about as well as anything else I heard. When we have lived with someone for years, we depend on them for many things. We understand each other and know what to expect from them in every area of life. When they are gone, it does leave a big hole, and we really miss them. But it is a relief that takes the edge off the grieving experience when we know, like King David, who grieved over the death of his baby, said, "I'll go to him but he will never return to me" (2 Samuel 12:23b, HCSB). We have the hope that we will see our loved ones again, and this does take some of the pain off our loss. As Paul said, "Death has been swallowed up in victory. Death, where is your victory? Death, where is your sting? Thanks be to God, who gives us the victory through our Lord Jesus Christ" (1 Corinthians 15:54–57).

One of the benefits Christians have over lost people who face the loss of loved ones is the fellowship of suffering from those who understand. These are people who can smile through their tears as they spend time with us during the dark hours. Thanks be to God for our church and the many Christian friends who spend time, write notes, and bring food during those sad times.

Notes

Good from Evil

How can good come from trouble, pain, injury, bed fastness, death, or loss? Put yourself in Joseph's shoes or sandals or whatever he had on his feet. He was beaten by his jealous brothers, thrown by them into a pit, and finally sold into slavery in Egypt.

It would have been a horrible experience even if it had been done by strangers, but by his brothers! His trouble didn't stop there. In Egypt he was in charge of everything in Potiphar's house, but even being a trustworthy servant and rejecting Potiphar's wife's advances got him thrown into prison. We know the story of how Joseph was freed from prison and how his whole family was finally rescued from starvation and given land to settle on in Egypt. It is a remarkable story of how God brought good from evil.

Romans 8:28 reminds us that God causes all things to work together for good to those who love Him and are called according to His purpose. Verse 29 gives us a clue about what God considers good. It says there that we are predestined to be conformed to the image of His Son. I assume this means that any experience that causes us to become more like Jesus is good in God's sight. Lying on our back in pain might make us more patient or give us a depth of understanding so that God can use us to minister to others.

Why would God tell us to give thanks in everything (1 Thessalonians 5:18) if it weren't possible for Him to bring good out of our worst experiences? One of the most difficult experiences for us is the death of a loved one. This is especially true if the death is premature. God tells us, "But we do not want you to be uninformed, brethren, about those who are asleep, that you may not to grieve, as do the rest who have no hope. For if we believe that Jesus died and rose again, even so God will bring with Him those who have fallen asleep in Jesus" (1 Thessalonians 4:13–14). He closes that passage by telling us to comfort one another with these words.

Death, which might be considered by the world to be the worst evil, is for the Christian not the end but the beginning of life in heaven with the Lord. That is the ultimate good.

There is a poem that speaks of walking with pleasure and then with sorrow. The poet learned nothing from pleasure but much from sorrow. Just think about it. When we are all excited about something and laughing and having a good time, how much serious thinking do we do?

On the other hand, when we run into trouble or some kind of difficulty, we do some really serious thinking. We think about our future. We look for help and discover how much friends mean to us. We get serious about our prayer life and discover the help that God alone can give. We find out or are reminded of what is really important in life.

There is an analogy from physical life. We gain strength from resistance. Some examples are lifting weights, doing pushups, and running. Hard times and losses are resistance in life. We learn from them. We learn to be more patient, and we develop understanding, sympathy, and compassion. We don't think about difficulties as good, but much good comes from them.

Notes

Grieve Not As Others Do

"But we do not want you to be uninformed, brethren, about those who are asleep, that you may not grieve, as do the rest who have no hope" (1 Thessalonians 4:13). Paul refers to death as sleep because it is not the end for those who have "fallen asleep in Jesus." Even so, it does not mean that all the pain and sense of loss vanish.

As Paul said, we don't grieve as "the rest who have no hope." He didn't say we don't grieve. Our grief is different from the grief of those who have no hope. When Carol, my first wife, died, I was comforted by reading this promise: "Let not your heart be troubled; believe in God, believe also in Me. In My Father's house are many dwelling places; if it were not so, I would have told you; and if I go and prepare a place for you, I will come again, and receive you to Myself; that where I am, there you may be also" (John 14:1–3).

In spite of this promise, "it leaves" as my niece wrote, "a big hole." C. S. Lewis[44] described it this way: "Grief still feels like fear. Perhaps, more strictly like suspense. Or like waiting; just hanging about waiting for something to happen. It gives life a permanent provisional feeling. It doesn't seem worth starting anything. I can't settle down. I yawn, I fidget. Up till this I always had too little time. Now there is nothing but time, almost pure time, and empty successiveness."

Obviously when we have lived for years with someone, nearly everything we do is done together. When that person dies, conversation is gone, eating together is gone, planning together is gone, going to places together is gone, and the giving and taking of advice is gone, All the things the other person did, the cooking, the cleaning, the lifting, the driving, the bookkeeping, the writing, the reminding, the shopping, the praying—all is gone. It does leave a big hole.

Still, our grief is very different. "For if we believe that Jesus died and rose again, even so God will bring with Him those who have fallen asleep in Jesus" (1 Thessalonians 4:14). We have the hope of seeing our loved ones again, and that makes a world of difference.

Our God is a God of comfort. "Blessed be the God and Father of our Lord Jesus Christ, the Father of mercies and God of all comfort; who comforts us in all of our afflictions so that we may be able to comfort those who are in any affliction with the comfort with which we ourselves are comforted by God" (2 Corinthian 1:3–4).

God does not want us to waste our experiences both good and bad. With His help, we can learn and grow so that out of our experiences, we can minister to others.

There is a poem that reminds us that life is a weaving where we see just the underside but God sees the upper side. We see only the present, but God knows the future. We see only a brief few years, but God sees eternity. If we could know what God knows, it would very likely moderate our grief and make it less painful.

Praise God! The source of all good.

Notes

HAPPINESS

The word *happy* appears in the New Testament just one time. It is in Romans and has a negative connotation in that it doesn't say how to be happy but how not to be unhappy. "The faith that you have, have as your own conviction before God. Happy is he who does not condemn himself in what he approves" (Romans 14:22). You are happy if you don't condemn yourself in what you approve. Sounds like you are happy if you can avoid a guilty conscience. When I was studying this, I thought perhaps the Bible's definition of happiness would be "contentment."

It turns out that the word *content* is found only five times in the New Testament. The meanings seem to say you should be content with what you have. Don't let what you don't have destroy your contentment: "And some soldiers were questioning Him, saying 'and what about us, what shall we do?' And He said to them, 'Do not take money from anyone by force, or accuse anyone falsely, and be content with your wages'" (Luke 3:14).

Paul had a physical problem that could have destroyed his contentment, but he found a way to overcome it. Jesus told him: "My grace is sufficient for you, for power is perfected in weakness" (2 Corinthians 12:9). "Therefore I am well content with weaknesses, with insults, with distresses, with persecutions, with difficulties, for Christ's sake; for when I am weak then I am strong" (2 Corinthians 12:10). Better to rely on Jesus' presence and power that on our own strength.

It sounds like to be content is to be happy. In the Old Testament the word *happy* occurs in Job: "Behold, how happy is the man whom God reproves, so do not despise the discipline of the Almighty" (Job 5:17). How strange that the word *happy* should appear in Job. If any man ever had reason to be unhappy, it would be Job.

Hebrews tells us the same thing: "My son, do not regard lightly the discipline of the Lord, Nor faint when you are being reproved by Him; for those whom the Lord loves He disciplines, and He scourges every son whom He receives" (Hebrews 12:5b–6). We should be happy because of God's discipline, because it is a sign that God loves us and that we have been accepted into His family. By the way, this is hard to understand and accept. My father paddled me quite a few times, but I never did think it was because he loved me. But then, Dad didn't spank our neighbor's children. God disciplines His own.

Our nation's Declaration of Independence includes "the pursuit of happiness" as one of our rights. Pursuing happiness doesn't sound like a biblical goal. Happiness is the result of being in the center of God's will. The Beatitudes tell us about how to be blessed: be poor in spirit, mourn, be gentle, seek God's righteousness, be merciful, be pure in heart, be peacemakers, and be the persecuted. Genuine happiness is found in the center of God's will.

Notes

HEAVEN

It is good to be reminded of the place where several of our friends and family are residents. C. S. Lewis[45] says, "If I find in myself a desire which no experience in this world can satisfy, the most probable explanation is that I was made for another world." It is true that God made us for Himself, but He created us so that we must choose Him; that way our relationship with Him is not artificial but genuine.

Our departed friends and family chose Him when they placed their faith in Jesus and were born again. This gave them spiritual life. Jesus said to the woman at the well, "God is spirit; and those who worship must worship in spirit and truth" (John 4:24). Once we have spiritual life, through the new birth experience, we are able to worship our heavenly Father and are given a passport to heaven.

It may be that God helps us look forward to heaven by designing us so that as we grow older and begin to experience aches and pains, we're less able to enjoy the earthly life. Paul said, "For our citizenship is in heaven, from which also we eagerly wait for a Savior, the Lord Jesus Christ; who will transform the body of our humble state into conformity with the body of His glory, by the exertion of the power that He has even to subject all things to Himself" (Philippians 3:20–21).

The body of His glory! After His resurrection Jesus walked through walls and was able to go from place to place, seemingly without the passing of time. Won't that be exciting, with all the aches, pains, and stiffness gone. I used to kid my wife, Carol, by suggesting that in heaven God would give us our own galaxy to govern, and that if I wanted to visit her, all I would have to do was wish to be there and in an instant I would be.

The apostle John gives us the best description of heaven: "And I saw a new heaven and a new earth; for the first heaven and the first earth passed away, and there is no longer any sea. And I saw the holy city, New Jerusalem, coming down out of heaven from God, made ready as a bride adorned for her husband. And I heard a loud voice from the throne, saying, 'Behold, the tabernacle of God is among men, and He shall dwell among them, and they shall be His people, and God Himself shall be among them, and He shall wipe away every tear from their eyes; and there shall no longer be any death; there shall no longer be any mourning, or crying, or pain; the first things have passed away'" (Revelation 21:1–4). This passage gives us great comfort.

The things on earth that are so painful will not exist in heaven. Separation, injury, rejection, cancer, deafness, blindness, physical disabilities, and weakness will not exist. Our new bodies will not have these undesirable features. No one will be slighted or inferior. There will be no robbers, murderers, sex offenders, or tyrants to bully or injure us.

We need to work at our witnessing. One thing I have not been able to understand is how we will be happy in heaven when some of our loved ones and friends don't make it there. Perhaps God gives us a blind spot in our memories.

Notes

KEEP ON LEARNING

Perhaps you are familiar with this verse that was the key verse for Baptist Training Union or, as we knew it, BTU. "Study to shew thyself approved unto God, a workman that needeth not to be ashamed, rightly dividing the Word of Truth" (2 Timothy 2:15, KJV). The New American Standard version begins with "Be diligent." Romans 12:2 challenges us "to not be conformed to this world, but be transformed by the renewing of our mind."

Proverbs has much to say about wisdom and understanding. "Buy truth, and do not sell it, Get wisdom and instruction and understanding" (Proverbs 23:23). "By wisdom a house is built, and by understanding it is established; and by knowledge the rooms are filled with all precious and pleasant riches" (Proverbs 24:3–4).

I wrote a little book titled *The Learning Team: The Learner, the Leader and the Library.* The theme of the book is that the *learner* is responsible. We can't learn for him. We can only help him. Before we can understand anything, we have to have enough accurate information about the subject. Learning occurs, at least in part, in the search for that information. We could say, "No searching, no learning."

What do you do when you study your Sunday school lesson and come across something you don't understand? Do you look for help in a Bible commentary? When you come across an unfamiliar word, do you reach for a dictionary? If we don't look, we don't learn.

When our three sons were in school and doing their homework, they would come to us with questions. Most of the time we would ask them if they had looked it up in the dictionary or encyclopedia. We expected them to do the searching before we gave them an answer. All of us should have some reference books in our home library.

The story of Benjamin Franklin is one of the best examples of the value of reading.

> At seventeen he was a poor, penniless runaway, walking the streets of Philadelphia. As Deborah Read smilingly watched her future husband walk by her door, eating a great loaf of bread he had just purchased with his last penny, she little dreamed that in a few years his companionship would be eagerly sought by the most cultured of three continents. He did not attend college in the interval, but enriched his mind by industriously employing every spare moment reading the

best authors. Books were his inseparable companions which were forever supplementing his own narrow experience. He became the greatest American diplomat of his day. When we remember that nearly all his wisdom was acquired through the practice of careful reading, a habit which he formed early in life, we can better understand why he often said, 'No man can be truly educated or successful in life unless he is a reader of books.'

One of the most interesting books I have read is *I Love Books* by John Snider.[46] The story of Franklin came from that book.

Do we have questions? Are we curious about anything? Finding answers and satisfying that curiosity makes life much more interesting. One benefit is that it gives us something to talk about other than weather, food, and people.

My first pastor, Elwyn Wilkinson, always had a book in his hand. If he had to wait for anything, he read. It is better to read something carefully chosen than a magazine from a table in the doctor's office. My son Bobby, a professor of statistics at the University of Tennessee, examines several books to decide what to read next. He wants to use his reading time on the most relevant material.

If you are in a church that has a good library, use it. Church libraries look for the best reading material. Readers don't have to wade through a bunch of mediocre material to find the good things.

Stay alive until the Lord calls you home. Keep on reading and learning.

Notes

Joy in the Faith

Paul said, "And convinced of this, I know that I shall remain and continue with you for all your progress and joy in the faith, so that your proud confidence in me may abound in Christ Jesus through my coming to you again" (Philippians 1:25–26). Apparently the Philippians were a very happy people.

"These things I have spoken to you, that in Me you may have peace. In the world you have tribulation, but take courage; I have overcome the world" (John 16:33). Some translations say, "Be of good cheer."

"Thou wilt make known to me the path of life; In Thy presence is fullness of joy; In Thy right hand there are pleasures forever" (Psalm 16:11). The word *joy* occurs 228 times in the Bible. That makes it a fairly important theme. *Joy* appears twenty-four times in the gospels. Jesus said, "These things I have spoken to you, that my joy may be in you, and that your joy may be full" (John 15:11). One of the gifts Jesus give us is His joy.

The word *cheer* doesn't appear very many times. Here is one we all know about: "God loves a cheerful giver" (2 Corinthians 9:7). The English word for the Greek word *cheerful* is *hilarious*. Ralph Earle in *Word Meanings in the New Testament*[47] says that "When the Lord's people give generously the Lord's blessing descends." I checked on *cheer* and *joy* in Random House Webster's College Dictionary and one word common to both is *happy*. Contentment would seem to be part of *joyful* and *cheerful*. A sour face or a grouchy attitude is out of place in the life of a Christian.

All of us enjoy a good laugh. It seems that laughter can even have a healing effect. Norman Cousins, a writer and peace advocate, actually healed himself by laughing a lot. How often have we experienced a tense situation that was relieved by someone who broke the ice with a word that caused everyone to laugh? We know that smiles and frowns affect us. Worry might cause ulcers.

What is the joy that Jesus gives us? There is certainly a lot to give us a sense of contentment. Because of our faith in the Christ who died on the cross for us, our sins are forgiven and they no longer come between us and God. God becomes our heavenly Father and Jesus our brother, and we have the continuous presence of the Holy Spirit in our lives to guide us, help us understand the Bible, prompt us in our prayer life, and convict us when we sin.

Our future in heaven is secure because we know that Jesus has gone to prepare a place for us and will come to receive us to Himself when we draw the last breath in this life.

In addition to all that, we have wonderful fellowship with Christian friends and a church where we can worship, learn, and serve.

Jesus gives us His joy. What a wonderful gift it is.

Notes

THE BODY OF CHRIST

"And He gave some as apostles, and some as prophets, and some as evangelists, and some as pastors and teachers" (Ephesians 4:11). This verse lists the workers that the Lord set apart to do His work in the world. As far as I know, we don't have apostles and prophets, but we do have evangelists and pastors. I understand that pastors and teachers are meant to be the same person.

Today we have evangelists, pastors, and associate pastors; music, youth, and preschool ministers; and others, depending on the size of the church. Verse 12 sets forth the responsibilities of these leaders: "for the equipping of the saints for the work of service, to the building up of the body of Christ" or, we could say, to the building up of the church, which is the body of Christ.

The equipping of the saints means that these ministers are to train us, the saints, to do the work of the church. It may be that to some extent, in some churches, the saints may have altered the plan so that the saints oversee the work of the ministers.

Here is an explanation of how the work is to be done: "but speaking the truth in love, we are to grow up in all aspects into Him, who is the head, even Christ, from whom the whole body, being fitted and held together by that which every joint supplies, according to the proper working of each individual part, causes the growth of the body for the building up of itself in love" (Ephesians 4:15–16). Each one of us is a part of the body. We are the hands, feet, arms, and legs. When these work together, as trained by the ministers, the church will grow.

Rick Warren's book[48] *The Purpose Driven Life* describes how each church member is to discover his or her spiritual gift and then put it to work building the church. Here are some of the spiritual gifts: "And since we have gifts that differ according to the grace given to us, let each exercise them accordingly; if prophecy, according to the proportion of his faith; if service, in his serving; or he who teaches, in his teaching; or he who exhorts, in his exhortation; he who gives with liberality; he who leads with diligence; he who shows mercy with cheerfulness" (Romans 12:6–8).

Paul writes, "And do not grieve the Holy Spirit of God by whom you were sealed for the day of redemption. Let all bitterness and wrath and anger and clamor and slander be put away from you, along with all malice. And be kind to one another, tender-hearted, forgiving each other, just as God in Christ also has forgiven you" (Ephesians 4:30–32). No church can grow if members are grieving the Holy Spirit. Members of the body must work together in a peaceful, coordinated way for the church to grow.

Jesus told Peter that he would build His church based on the faith that Peter had expressed at Caesarea Philippi: "He said to them, 'But who do you say that I am?' and Simon Peter answered and said, 'Thou art the Christ, the son of the living God.' And Jesus answered and said to him, 'Blessed are you, Simon Barjona, because flesh and blood did not reveal this to you, but My Father who is in heaven. And I also say to you that you are Peter, and upon this rock I will build My church and the gates of Hades shall not overpower it'" (Matthew 16:15–18). Peter's confession, his faith in Christ, was the rock, not Peter himself.

The church is the body of Christ of which He is the head: "To the building up of the body of Christ" (Ephesians 4:12b). "To Him be the glory in the church and in Christ Jesus to all generations forever and ever. Amen" (Ephesians 3:21).

Notes

The Tongue

The Bible has more than 100 references to the tongue, many of which are warnings. "If anyone thinks himself to be religious, and yet does not bridle his tongue but deceives his own heart, this man's religion is worthless" (James 1:26). The tongue sometimes seems to act independently from our brain. We blurt out our words without thinking about the consequences.

"But no one can tame the tongue; it is a restless evil and full of deadly poison. With it we bless our Lord and Father; and with it we curse men, who have been made in the likeness of God; from the same mouth come both blessing and cursing. My brethren, these things ought not to be this way" (James 3:8–10). We blame the tongue, but the tongue is just the tool or instrument of our mind.

It isn't the tongue that criticizes and compliments. It is the instrument that expresses what we are thinking. It is our thought life or our attitude that needs attention. There are times when we should compliment someone if the compliment is called for and sincere. If it is not sincere but flattery, it is a form of a lie.

There are times when we have criticized someone because of our own impatience. Afterward we wish we had kept our mouth shut. If we truly want to love our neighbor, we must learn to control our tongue.

There are many ways to tell lies: exaggeration, leaving out details, or winking. Anytime we alter the truth by leaving out a word or changing the tone of our voice, we leave a wrong impression; we have lied.

Our tongue is the instrument that conveys all these false impressions, half-truths, and outright lies. There have been times when we wish we had bitten our tongue to keep it under control.

Christian love compels us to work on our speech. What we say is just an indication of what is in our heart. James speaks to this: "Does a fountain send out from the same opening both fresh and bitter water? Can a fig tree, my brethren, produce olives, or a vine produce figs? Neither can salt water produce fresh" (James 3:11–12).

This is saying to us that our speech betrays what is in our heart. When we sincerely desire a positive influence on people, we won't pass on rumors or say things that diminish them in the eyes of others.

It really comes down to controlling our tongue.

But James has just said, in chapter 3, verse 8, that no man can control the tongue. True, man by himself cannot do it. We need

God's help. "But the wisdom from above is first pure, then peaceable, gentle, reasonable, full of mercy and good fruits, unwavering, without hypocrisy" (James 3:17).

Staying in touch with God through Bible study, prayer, and worship is the only way we can control the tongue and make it an instrument of blessing instead of blight on our testimony.

Notes

With All Your Heart

"You shall love the Lord your God with all your heart, and with all your soul, and with all your mind" (Matthew 22:37, Mark 12:30, and Luke 10:27). Mark and Luke add, "With all your strength." There is an emphasis in the Bible on giving ourselves to the Lord in a complete and enthusiastic way. The word *all* occurs in Scripture about 5,400 times.

Here are a few of the *alls*: *all the good, all the peace, all times, all places, all your men, all the saints, all the people, all of you, all the brethren, all those, all the days.* It seems that where God is concerned, all of lots of things are involved. *With all our hearts* certainly includes the idea of enthusiasm about our involvement in God's work.

This experience was mentioned earlier but it applies here as well. After I began as minister of education at the Immanuel Baptist Church in Lexington, Kentucky, several men paid my way to take a Dale Carnegie course. The course involved remembering names and speaking. Part of the speech training involved making a newspaper shillelagh and tearing it to shreds by beating it on the table in front of me while making a one-minute speech. I was supposed to be angry or enthusiastic about the subject of the speech. I wasn't an enthusiastic person and I didn't anger easily. I had read about a drunk driver who had run over a little girl and decided I could get mad at that. When I began to speak, I acted angry, but as I beat on the table with the paper, my faked anger became genuine. In less than one minute what was artificial became real. The point of the story is that if we are not an enthusiastic person, we can act excited about something and the genuine emotion will develop.

Our service, our worship, and our giving can all be done with a degree of excitement and enthusiasm: as with all our heart. Titus tells us that Jesus "gave Himself for us to be His people who are zealous for good deeds" (Titus 2:14). Paul advises us, "Whatever you do, do your work heartily, as for the Lord rather than for men" (Colossians 3:23). First Peter 3:13 says, "And who is there to harm you if you prove zealous for what is good?"

I would challenge us to think about our involvement in church life and in the good things we do in our community; let's put as much zeal into it as we can. I used to run up stairs, but now I step slowly. I still get tired, but I won't use the elevator until I have to. If we aren't careful, we'll let age and infirmity hold us back more than necessary.

Let's not lose our zeal for the Lord and His work. When we can no longer go physically, we can pray zealously, study the Word eagerly, and love the Lord with all our heart.

Notes

Our Ministry

What is our responsibility as children of God, as believers in Christ, as members of the body of Christ, the church? There are many clues and commands that tell us what we should be and do. One of the clearest descriptions is in Ephesians: "And He gave some as apostles, and some as prophets, and some as evangelists, and some as pastors and teachers, for the equipping of the saints for the work of service, to the building up of the body of Christ; until we all attain to the unity of the faith, and of the knowledge of the Son of God, to a mature man, to the measure of the stature which belongs to the fullness of Christ" (Ephesians 4:11–13).

This tells us that it is the pastor's job to train us to do the work of building up the church. Some people seem to think it is the pastor's responsibility to reach people and minister to them, but it says here that it is his job to train us to do that work. It is the members of the body, the saints, who are responsible for building up the body of Christ, the church. It is sad when members think it is their job to tell the preacher what to do.

Building up the body certainly includes adding new members. The Great Commission in Matthew tells us to make disciples. Witnessing for Christ and winning the lost to Him is our first priority.

Another dimension of our responsibility is described in Galatians: "So then, while we have opportunity, let us do good to all men and especially to those who are of the household of faith" (Galatians 6:10). This is saying that church members should help each other. What does "do good" mean? It certainly doesn't mean "to do evil" or "to do nothing."

Then James gets very specific: "This is pure and undefiled religion in the sight of our God and Father, to visit orphans and widows in their distress, and to keep oneself unstained by the world" (James 1:27). Churches have many people in nursing homes, and fellow members are responsible for visiting them. It is far better for Christians to take care of people than it is for the government to do it. When Christians help, there is a witness who can turn people to the Lord. For many people, the need for this is greater than their physical or psychological need.

God gives each of His children at least one spiritual gift. When these gifts are put to work in the body of Christ, the church prospers in every way. In the center of his discourse on spiritual gifts, Paul gave us the chapter on love. Whatever we do as members of the body of Christ, our actions and words are to be controlled by a spirit of love.

Jesus told us about the man in the ditch and the Samaritan who helped him. In Matthew 25 Jesus gave us a list of people needing help: the hungry, the thirsty, the stranger, the naked, the sick, and the prisoner.

He condemned those who failed to help and praised those who helped. What would Jesus have to say about us?

Notes

Struggles in Life, Hope for the Future

The restricting cocoon and the struggle required for a butterfly to escape it is God's way of forcing fluid from the body of the butterfly into its wings, so that it will be able to fly once it is free from the cocoon.

The struggle gives the butterfly the strength needed for flight. In a similar way, the difficulties and problems we face in life may be God's way of making us strong. "Consider it all joy, my brethren, when you encounter various trials, knowing that the testing of your faith produces endurance" (James 1:2–3).

The complete change when a butterfly emerges from its cocoon reminds us of the change that takes place in our life when we repent of our sin and trust Christ for salvation. Paul puts it this way: "Therefore if any man is in Christ, he is a new creature; the old things passed away; behold, new things have come" (2 Corinthians 5:17). This is the change that takes place during our earthly life, but there is more to come.

"But we do not want you to be uninformed, brethren, about those who are asleep, that you may not grieve, as do the rest who have no hope. For if we believe that Jesus died and rose again, even so God will bring with Him those who have fallen asleep in Jesus. For this we say to you by the word of the Lord, that we who are alive, and remain until the coming of the Lord, shall not precede those who have fallen asleep. For the Lord Himself will descend from heaven with a shout, with the voice of the archangel, and with the trumpet of God; and the dead in Christ will rise first. Then we who are alive and remain shall be caught up together with them in the clouds to meet the Lord in the air, and thus we shall always be with the Lord. Therefore comfort one another with these words" (1 Thessalonians 4:13–18).

Jesus' resurrection is the hope, the proof, the guarantee, and the portrait of our future. The body that Jesus had after the resurrection was different. Though He ate and talked and was recognized by His followers, He walked through walls. He didn't need a door. Later his followers saw Him ascend into heaven. This was a picture of how someday He would return.

And what of the change to come? Listen to what God has to say to us: "Behold, I tell you a mystery; we shall not all sleep, but we shall all be changed, in a moment, in the twinkling of an eye, at the last trumpet; for the trumpet will sound, and the dead will be raised imperishable, and we shall be changed.—But thanks be to God, who gives us the victory through our Lord Jesus Christ. Therefore, my beloved brethren, be steadfast, immovable, always abounding in the work of the Lord, knowing that your toil is not in vain in the Lord" (1 Corinthians 15:51–52 and 57–58).

When my first wife, Carol, died, I found great comfort in this promise: "for I go to prepare a place for you. And if I go and prepare a place for you, I will come again, and receive you to Myself; that where I am, there you may be also" (John 14:2b–3). When we are faced with loss in this life, there is no greater source of comfort than God's word.

Only those who know Christ as Savior have this hope for a glorious future, with a body not wracked with pain, a reunion with family and friends, and an eternity in the presence of God.

Notes

THE ROMAN ROAD

The Roman Road is a collection of verses from the book of Romans that are used to present the gospel to an unsaved person. There may be more than one such road, but I am familiar with the one that follows.

It begins with the fact that everyone has sinned: "For all have sinned and fall short of the glory of God" (Romans 3:23). Romans quotes Psalm 14: "There is none righteous, not even one" (Romans 3:10). In all of mankind, from Adam until now, there has not been a person who has not sinned except our Lord Jesus Christ.

No person has ever been able to have a relationship with God whose sin has not been dealt with. It has to be gotten out of the way, because God cannot associate with sin.

God has made a way: "For the wages of sin is death, but the free gift of God is eternal life in Christ Jesus our Lord" (Romans 6:23). The death spoken of here is eternal separation from God. In the afterlife there are only two places to be: heaven and hell. Heaven is where God is, and no sin is allowed there.

How is the free gift of God acquired? "But God demonstrates His own love toward us, in that while we were yet sinners, Christ died for us" (Romans 5:8). Christ took upon Himself the sin of the entire world. His sacrificial death paid the price. Only God knows how this could be. It is enough to know that sin is a serious matter with God because of the harm that it does to His creation.

Man's need is a new heart. He needs a spiritual heart. He needs a heart that is tuned to God. He receives that heart when he comes to Jesus: "But what does it say? The Word is near you and in your mouth and in your heart"—that is, the word of faith which we are preaching, that if you confess with your mouth Jesus as Lord, and believe in your heart that God raised Him from the dead, you shall be saved; for with heart man believes, resulting in righteousness, and with mouth he confesses, resulting in salvation" (Romans 10:8–10).

The promise in verse 13 is more to the point: "Whoever will call on the name of the Lord will be saved" (Roman 10:13). Once we turn to God in faith, He gives us a new heart and a new life that listens to God and is able to better control the deeds of the flesh. We open the door of our heart to Him and He gladly enters in. The gift, spoken of earlier, is Christ's sinless life that God now sees when He looks upon us.

> Saved by His power divine,
> Saved to new life sublime!
> Life now is sweet and my joy is complete,
> For I'm saved, saved, saved.

Notes

A Special Creation

Think about Earth with all its resources and its special location in the universe. Then consider man with his capabilities to use Earth's natural resources. To think that it all came about by chance and natural processes requires more faith than to believe what the Bible has to say about it.

The first chapter of John begins by saying, "In the beginning was the Word, and the Word was with God, and the Word was God. He was in the beginning with God. All things came into being by Him; and apart from Him nothing came into being that has come into being" (John 1:1–3). He not only made everything, but according to Paul in Colossians, He maintains the entire creation. "He is before all things, and in Him **all things hold together**" (Colossians 1:17). I have heard that scientists have a theory called the **Colossians theory**. In the heart of an atom the positive charges should repel each other like the south ends of two magnets repel each other. Instead they are held together with a mighty force. The theory is based on Colossians 1:17.

The book of Psalms has David asking, "What is man that Thou dost take thought of him? And the son of man, that Thou dost care for him? Yet thou hast made him a little lower than God, and dost crown him with glory and majesty! Thou dost make him to rule over the works of thy hands; thou hast put all things under his feet" (Psalm 8:4–6).

The word *man* appears in the Bible about 2,100 times. God has delegated to man the responsibility of caring for His creation. He made us with minds, hands, and eyes that enable us to understand, appreciate, and manipulate the elements of His creation. Without man and his abilities, all the beauty and usability of Earth and the universe would have no purpose.

I have never read this anywhere, but I think that it requires the entire universe of galaxies and stars to maintain the stability of Earth. Any way you look at it, humans and Earth are special. Earth really is unique. Days vary in length because Earth tilts on its axis. The tilt is caused by the moon's gravity, and the amount of tilt is caused by the size of the moon. The tilt gives Earth its seasons. The moon gives us our tides and ocean currents, which in turn regulate our climate. If we had no moon, we wouldn't be here. A smaller or larger moon would not give the conditions favorable to life.

"In the beginning God created the heavens and the earth. And God made the two great lights, the greater light to govern the day, and the lesser light to govern the night; He made the stars also" (Genesis 1:1, 16). Just five words are devoted to the creation of billions of galaxies and stars.

Earth and man are *special*! It should make us bow down and praise God, who created us and everything that exists.

Notes

THE CURE FOR ANXIETY

Matthew devotes ten verses to this subject and concludes with "Therefore do not be anxious for tomorrow; for tomorrow will care for itself. Each day has enough troubles of its own" (Matthew 6:34). This is an admonition to live one day at a time. Anxiety and thinking are two different processes.

It would not be wise to not think about the future. I look ahead and mark my calendar for the things that I will need to do in the days ahead. That process is not being anxious about the future. Having a file system that get us ready to prepare a tax return, when the time comes for that process, is not worrying about tomorrow.

Anxiety is dwelling on events and problems that may or may not happen in the days ahead. It is fretting over the future to the neglect of things that need our attention today.

Saving for the future is not worrying about the future. Preparing for the future is not being anxious about the future. The person who is too extravagant in spending today, to the neglect of saving for tomorrow, is not being wise. Doing nothing, making no plans or preparation for the years ahead, is being presumptuous. To do so would result in others, who had prepared for the future, having to take care of us.

I like the Living Bible's treatment of Philippians 4:6: "Do not worry about anything instead pray about everything and don't forget to thank God for His answers."

When we dwell on what may or may not happen tomorrow, we may neglect what needs our attention today. It is much better to pray about our concerns and leave them to the Lord. Worry saps our energy and distracts our attention from dealing with things that need our attention now, the things that we can do something about today.

Worry is a sin. Worry represents a lack of faith in our Heavenly Father. Jesus reminds us that, if the Father takes care of the birds of the air and the grass of the fields, He will do much more for us.

Looking back and fretting over something that happened in the past is a waste of time and energy. The same is true of looking ahead and *dwelling* on something that may or may not happen.

God would have us do a good job of taking care of today. Our first priority is our testimony. What kind of influence are we on our family, friends and neighbors? An optimistic outlook on the future and an obvious faith in the Father is a lot better influence than a frowning fretting attitude about what may or may not happen tomorrow.

Worry is like a rocking chair. It keeps you busy but it gets you nowhere.

Notes

FINALLY

Paul admonishes the brethren: "Rejoice in the Lord always; again I say rejoice! Let your forbearing spirit be known to all men" (Philippians 4:4–5a). To be forbearing meant that they were gentle, considerate, thoughtful, and gracious. These would be real nice people to be around.

Then, he said, "Be anxious for nothing, but in everything by prayer and supplication with thanksgiving let your requests be made know to God" (Philippians 4:6). They were not to worry about anything but instead were to pray about everything.

If all of this were true, they would enjoy the peace of God, which was so wonderful that it was beyond understanding. This peace of God would guard their hearts and minds in Christ Jesus. Once our hearts and minds are safe, nothing in this life can threaten us.

After all of this Paul said, "Finally, brethren, whatever is true, whatever is honorable, whatever is right, whatever is pure, whatever is lovely, whatever is of good repute, if there is any excellence and if anything worthy of praise, let your mind dwell on these things" (Philippians 4:8).

If we practice all of this, we can expect the God of peace to be with us. What is Paul talking about when he says, "Finally"? He is talking about our minds—what we think about and talk about.

We must be careful to tell the truth. Sometimes we pass along information without knowing whether it is totally true. I know that my memory is not all that good and that if I'm not careful, my description of an event will not be all that accurate.

Our conversation should be about whatever is honorable, right, pure, and lovely. There are some things that just don't need to be repeated.

Leslie Flynn in his book *Did I Say That?*[49] tells about Madame Curie, the genius who discovered radium. "After the untimely death of her husband she bravely continued her work. Then subdued whispers began to circulate. Naturally, a few men were close friends in her laboratories, producing radium for the human race. The whispers grew to widely publicized terrible stories, gross lies. The untruths cut deep until the lonely, brokenhearted widow actually contemplated suicide! She never did recuperate fully from the assault of the whispering tongues."

We are to think about things of good repute, things that are excellent and worthy of praise. Look for the good in people. Look for the good things in our church services. What do we talk about at our church suppers? Is it the tough meat or the great salad bar and the delicious dessert?

Laughter and positive thoughts and speech are good for our health.

Paul reminds us that if we want to enjoy the peace that God gives, then we are to follow the formula spelled out in Philippians after the word *finally.*

Notes

REFERENCES

[1]   Clifton J. Allen, *the Broadman Bible Commentary,* Vol. 9 (Nashville, TN: Broadman Press, 1970), p. 361.

[2]   Dallas Willard, *Divine Conspiracy* (New York: HarperCollins, 1997), p. 307.

[3]   Pete Briscoe, *Belief Matters* (Eugene, OR: Harvest House, 2009), p. 7.

[4]   Wesley L. Forbis, ed., *the Baptist Hymnal* (Nashville, TN: Convention Press, 1991), p. 161.

[5]   W. R. White, *Baptist Distinctives* (Nashville, TN: Convention Press, 1946), p. 19.

[6]   White, p. 21.

[7]   Dr. Paul Brand, *Fearfully and Wonderfully Made* (Grand Rapids, MI: Zondervan Publishing House, 1980), p. 46.

[8]   Herschel H. Hobbs, *The Baptist Faith and Message* (Nashville, TN: Convention Press, 1971), chapter 6.

[9]   C. B. Hogue, *the Doctrine of Salvation* (Nashville, TN: Convention Press, 1978), p. 87.

[10] Hogue, p. 93.

[11] Hogue, p. 120.

[12] Leslie B. Flynn, *19 Gifts of the Spirit* (Wheaton, IL: Victor Books, 1994).

[13] Hobbs, p. 100.

[14] Hobbs, p. 38.

[15] Forbis, p. 2.

[16] Forbis, p. 261.

[17] Rick Warren, *The Purpose Driven Life* (Grand Rapids, MI: Zondervan, 2002).

18 Flynn.

19 Dovie Jones, *Christian Poems* (New York: Vantage Press: 1971), p. 30.

20 Hobbs, p. 117.

21 Robert Gange, *Origins and Destiny* (Nashville, TN: Word Publishers, 1986).

22 Robert Gentry, *Creation's Tiny Mystery* (Knoxville, TN: Earth Science Associates, 1986).

23 Forbis, p. 187.

24 Leslie B. Flynn, *Did I Say That* (Nashville, TN: Broadman Press, 1959), p. 26.

25 Clifton J. Allen, Vol. 1, p. 416.

26 Ralph Sockman, *the Higher Happiness* (Nashville, TN: Abingdon-Cokesbury Press, 1950).

27 Forbis, p. 142.

28 Wayne Martindale, *the Quotable Lewis* (Wheaton, IL: Tyndale House Publishers, 1990), p. 579.

29 Dovie Jones, p. 137.

30 Forbis, p. 350.

31 Gallop.com/poll/14788.

32 Harold Dye, *Through God's Eyes* (Nashville, TN: Broadman Press, 1947), p. 29 – 43. Used with permission.

33 Dye, p, 42 – 43.

34 Dye, p. 45.

35 Dye, p. 67.

36 Dye, p. 85.

37 Forbis, p. 2.

38 Lincoln quoted from the Internet. Go to Bing and type Lincoln's "Nowhere else to turn."

39 Martindale, p. 168.

40 Allen, Vol. 8, p. 176.

41 William Evans, *the Great Doctrines of the Bible* (Chicago, IL: Moody Press), p. 236.

42 From the Internet. Use Bing Web search.

43 James Hastings, *Dictionary of the Bible* (New York: Charles Scribner's Sons, 1951), p. 950.

44 Martindale, p. 275.

45 Martindale, p. 287.

[46] John D. Snider, *I Love Books* (Washington, DC: Review and Herald, 1942), p. 59–60.

[47] Ralph Earle, *Word Meanings in the New Testament* (Kansas City, MO: Beacon Hill Press, 1986), p. 259.

[48] Warren, p. 227.

[49] Flynn, p. 26.

ABOUT THE AUTHOR

Keith Mee was born in Grants Pass, Oregon. He attended schools in Medford, Oregon, and graduated from high school in Richmond, California. After a semester at the University of California, Berkeley, he was drafted in 1943 and spent thirty-nine months in the army. While in the army, after basic training at Camp Walters, Texas, he entered the Army Specialized Training Program at the University of Kentucky, in Lexington.

While in Lexington he met Carol Jean Terry, who later became his wife. After a semester at the university, he was sent back to the infantry and overseas with the Seventy-first Infantry Division. When the war with Germany ended, the Seventy-first was in Austria. He was ushered out of the army in May 1946. After a year at the University of California at Berkeley, he moved back to Lexington, married Carol, and resumed school at the University of Kentucky, pursuing a degree in mechanical engineering.

Keith and Carol moved to Georgetown, Kentucky where Carol was employed as a home economics teacher at Garth High School. While in Georgetown they directed an Intermediate Training Union Department at the First Baptist Church. While commuting to the University of Kentucky, Keith also taught woodshop at Garth High.

After two years in Georgetown, Keith and Carol moved to Lexington, where Keith taught mechanical drawing, geography, consumer math, and driver training at Henry Clay High School. They were members of the Immanuel Baptist Church, where both taught in the University Sunday School Department. Keith was Training Union director and Carol was president of the Women's Missionary Union. Keith changed his major from mechanical engineering to education.

During a study of *Every Christian's Job,* by C. E. Mathews, Keith felt called to full-time Christian service. At the time, he was finishing his master's degree in education at the University of Kentucky. On June 1, 1952, Keith began serving as minister of education at Immanuel Baptist Church. He served in that capacity with three pastors: Elwyn Wilkinson, Wayne Todd, and H. B. Khunle.

After Keith spent eight years as minister of education, Wayne Todd, who had gone to the Baptist Sunday School Board as secretary of the Church Library Service, invited him to come to the board to supervise the Field Services Section. Over the next thirty years, until retirement on March 1, 1990, Keith supervised the work of five to seven consultants, conducted conferences, oversaw the setting up and operation of media centers at Ridgecrest and Glorieta, and wrote books and articles. At the same time, at Two Rivers Baptist Church in Nashville, he served as deacon chairman on seven occasions, served as pulpit committee chairman, taught a Sunday school class, and was librarian for thirty-five years.

He is author of the books *The Learner, the Leader and the Library; How to Use Audiovisuals; Promotion Ideas; More Promotion Ideas*; booklets *Yokefellow: the Deacon's Helper;* and *Developing Skills in Learning;* and 125 magazine articles. He wrote a chapter for *Christian Education Foundations for the Future*, published in 1991 by Moody Press.

In retirement he has continued to help churches develop their libraries. He is president of the Tennessee Church Library Affinity Team and church library team leader in the Knox County Association of Baptists. He and his wife, Jean, direct a senior adult Sunday school department at the Central Baptist Church of Bearden in Knoxville. The devotionals in this book were presented in the opening assembly of their Sunday school department.

Keith had three sons with Carol, who died in 2003. He married Jean Evans in 2005. Jean has a son and a daughter; her daughter died in 2011. Together Jean and Keith have twenty-six grandchildren and six great-grandchildren.

Keith's hobbies are rock collecting, rock tumbling, and woodworking. He and Jean enjoy making and giving away bookends and pen holders made of wood decorated with polished rocks.

CPSIA information can be obtained at www.ICGtesting.com
Printed in the USA
LVOW130101060612

284747LV00002B/3/P